The United States of Europe

Ernest Wistrich

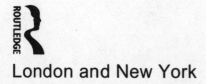

London and New York

First published 1994
by Routledge
11 New Fetter Lane, London EC4P 4EE

Simultaneously published in the USA and Canada
by Routledge
29 West 35th Street, New York, NY 10001

© 1994 Ernest Wistrich

Typeset in Baskerville by
ROM-Data Corporation, Falmouth, Cornwall, England.

Printed and bound in Great Britain by
Clays Ltd, St Ives plc

British Library Cataloguing in Publication Data

A catalogue record for this book is available from the British
Library.

*Library of Congress Cataloging in Publication Data has been
applied for.*

ISBN 0-415-09324-4 (pbk)

Contents

Preface

Three terms have been used over the last fifty years to describe the aims of European integration. First, there is the 'United States of Europe', used by Winston Churchill in several of his speeches in the 1940s calling for European unification. Jean Monnet, one of united Europe's founding fathers, promoted the objective through his Action Committee for a United States of Europe. The term 'European federation' was first used during the Second World War by federalist organisations such as Federal Union in Britain and the European Union of Federalists on the Continent. After the war, French foreign minister, Robert Schuman, in launching his project for the European Coal and Steel Community, described it as the first step in 'laying the foundations of a European federation'. The third term 'European Union' has come into common usage with the Rome Treaty, setting up the European Economic Community. This resolved 'to lay the foundations of an ever closer union among the peoples of Europe'. It is also the title given to the Maastricht Treaty.

All three terms have been employed without much of a clear distinction between them, which, if examined, is more semantic than of substance. They all describe a Europe united on federal lines: that is, not as a centralised unitary state but a union of states that retain autonomous powers over all issues that have not specifically been agreed by its member states to be exercised in common. The responsibilities that are pooled within the existing European Community are carried out by common institutions under Community laws, enacted by them, and taking precedence over national legislation. The distribution of powers between the European and national levels, agreed within treaties or amendments to them, are subject to interpretation and ultimate adjudication by the

European Court of Justice, which has the final word on these issues.

The title of this book was chosen to emphasise the federal definition of a union in which several states constitute a political unity while remaining independent as to all internal affairs, not transferred to its federal level. The title is not, however, to be understood as being based on the model of the United States of America. Federal systems vary throughout the world, depending on their origins and distinct cultural backgrounds. None of them can be regarded as the correct model for the United States of Europe, which is developing according to its own logic and circumstances.

The federal concept is well understood throughout Europe with the notable exception of the United Kingdom, where it is often perversely described as a centralised and unitary system of government – quite contrary to its true definition. The intense dislike of the 'f' word by some within the British establishment, together with their misconception of its meaning, explains the British government's opposition to its use. At Maastricht in December 1991, the British prime minister, John Major, fought tooth and nail against describing the proposed European Union as having a 'federal vocation'. Britain's partners were puzzled as, for them, the European Community from its inception was intended to pursue a federal goal. In the end a compromise was reached by dropping the word 'federal' and adopting 'an ever closer union of the European peoples in which decisions are taken as close to citizens as possible'. Responsibilities were to be allocated according to the principle of subsidiarity, under which the Community shall only take action which cannot effectively be achieved by the member states alone.

In Britain, part of the confusion over the definition of a European federation stemmed from a speech by its former prime minister, Margaret Thatcher, delivered in Bruges in 1988. She claimed that a federation would 'try to suppress nationhood and concentrate power at the centre of a European conglomerate' and would fit individual member countries 'into some sort of identikit European personality'. This claim was of course a total travesty. Indeed the word 'union' preferred by the British is more likely to imply a centralised system, whereas the 'federal goal' represents a hard commitment to a binding constitution within which the distribution of powers between the centre and its member states is fixed. Thus a United States of Europe or a European federation, based on the principle of subsidiarity, is the best guarantee of national identities and of the right to take national or subnational decisions which have not been explicitly transferred to the federal institutions – much better than a system of supposedly independent states which, without a constitution, would inevitably be dominated by the strongest.

The real conflict is between two diametrically opposed groups. First, there are those for whom European unity is characterised by a partnership between supranational institutions with defined powers and component states retaining their distinct identities and autonomies. Then there are others who are fundamentally opposed to any supranational powers and wish to base European unity on voluntary cooperation between totally sovereign and independent states. The European Community, which Britain joined, has from its origins been a supranational entity and not the free trade area so much preferred by the opponents of European integration. The account that follows explains the origins of integration, its development and its likely future evolution.

Chapter 1

The meaning of Maastricht

Over the last half century there has been greater change than over the preceding 500 years. The technological revolution has radically altered the nature of the world. The indiscriminate exploitation of natural resources and the uncontrolled use of them in some countries is having a global effect. Our common environment and the world's climate are under serious threat. Nuclear accidents, like Chernobyl, could make large parts of our planet uninhabitable for thousands of years. Nuclear weapons threaten the very survival of humanity, were they ever to be used. Even without their use, the threat of armed conflict in further-ance of foreign policy objectives, for centuries held to be the prerogative of states, has become increasingly obsolete. The mass-ive growth of international trade and its accompanying huge capital flows, and the emergence of multinational corporations, with annual turnovers often in excess of the gross national prod-ucts of independent countries, have made the whole world economically interdependent. As a result countries that try to isolate themselves by erecting barriers against the outside would pay a heavy price in economic stagnation and backwardness, while the rest of the world moves ahead.

These dramatic changes in the nature of global society have thrown up new problems that can no longer be tackled by indi-vidual countries merely looking after their own interests. Unfettered national sovereignty is obsolete, and economic and political independence is giving way to growing interdependence between nation states. The major task for the world today is to devise policies to deal with global problems and create appropri-ate political structures to ensure that the policies are put into effect. The same applies to individual continents or major regions within them that are affected by common problems. Among these such problems as pollution, disease, crime and terrorism know no frontiers and can no longer be tackled by individual countries in isolation, but require international solutions.

If total independence and unfettered sovereignty of nation states is becoming outdated, how should the world be organised? Merging individual countries into larger states with common governments is no answer. Most nations wish to preserve their distinct identities, languages and cultures. At the same time as democracy and active citizen participation grows, so does resentment against over-centralised national governments and distant authority exercised over people's daily lives. Local communities and regions within countries demand devolution of power so that they can deal with their problems at their level, instead of leaving it to faceless national bureaucrats, less aware of and less sensitive to local needs and wishes.

THE FEDERAL PATH

The only flexible answer to these seemingly conflicting trends is the adoption of federal solutions to accommodate them. The essence of federalism lies in the decentralisation of power wherever needs can be satisfied at lower levels of government, closer to those who are affected by them. Although federations take many different forms, generally they have emerged to unite separate states in a way in which powers exercised at federal level are confined to those that need common solutions and management. Most federal constitutions guarantee maximum autonomy and self-government to their component parts. The general principle is that federal government can only exercise those responsibilities which cannot be effectively fulfilled at lower tiers of government.

The European Community was founded to deal with the changing political and economic world and has advanced quite far along the federal road towards a European Union, which is its explicit objective. Its legal status stems from a constitution based on the treaties that set up the Community and from their subsequent amendments. The constitution and Community laws are binding on member states. The European Community is governed by an independent executive in the form of the European Commission. This is answerable to a directly elected European

Parliament which has powers to dismiss it. Community laws, which take precedence over national legislation, are formulated by the Commission and, after being subjected to formal consultation by the European Parliament, are enacted by the Council of Ministers, representing member governments.

The rapidly changing world has faced the European Community and its member countries with new challenges which require common action. That is why the Community is constantly evolving and acquiring new responsibilities and powers. Major reforms to the original treaties have most recently been enacted by two substantial revisions. The first was the Single European Act (SEA), which came into force in 1987. The second was the Maastricht Treaty on European Union signed in February 1992.

THE SINGLE EUROPEAN ACT

The Single European Act laid down that, for all practical purposes, national frontiers between the twelve member states of the European Community would disappear by the beginning of 1993. People, goods, services and capital would move as freely between Glasgow and Naples, Copenhagen and Lisbon or Dublin and Athens as between London and Manchester, Berlin and Munich or Paris and Lyon. The objective was to create a single European economy that would be more dynamic, faster growing, creating millions of new jobs and able to compete on more equal terms with the USA and Japan.

When the Treaty of Rome established the European Economic Community in 1958 one of its objectives was to set up a common market without customs barriers, primarily to improve the living standards of its citizens. The creation of the Common Market had dramatic results. Between 1958 and 1972 the economies of the six member states of the Community grew much faster than that of the USA, the world's richest country. Britain, more prosperous than any of the Six when they started, had been overtaken by all except Italy by the time it joined the Community fifteen years later. The progressive removal of the customs barriers and the development of closer economic relations between member states stimulated growth and accelerated the growth of living standards throughout the Community.

Following the oil crisis in 1973 and the subsequent recessions, progress in Europe slowed down and even halted. Yet the European

Community's principal competitors, the USA, Japan, and the emerging industrial economies of the Far East, continued to forge ahead. Europe's record on productivity, innovation, inflation, unemployment, and new job creation was poor. Increasingly the competitors' products priced European goods even out of Europe's own domestic markets, let alone the rest of the world. Relative impoverishment stared Europe in the face and something had to been done.

Various studies showed that, after its highly successful economic growth rate of 4.6 per cent per annum between 1960 and 1973, the European Community's growth fell by 50 per cent to an average of 2.3 per cent per annum. The reason for the dramatic decline was largely the Community's response to the economic crises of the 1970s. Instead of uniting to safeguard their futures, each country pursued its own individual protective policies and thus raised new barriers which inhibited trade between them. The cost of these barriers was formidable. The most authoritative estimate was produced for the European Commission in 1988 by the so-called Cecchini Report on the 'Cost of non-Europe' (Cecchini 1988). It showed that the overall cost of all non-tariff barriers was some Ecu 200 billion (£130 billion), equivalent to about 5 per cent of the Community's gross domestic product. The barriers included onerous customs formalities, exclusive national purchasing policies, differing standards for goods and services, and uncoordinated and often competing research and technological development. All these restrictions to trade had to go if Europe was to become competitive again.

To meet this challenge Lord Cockfield, then vice-president of the European Commission, proposed reforms in a White Paper (EC Commission 1985b) which set out nearly 300 measures that needed to be enacted by the end of 1992, to remove virtually all internal Community barriers to the free movement of people, goods, services and capital and thus create a single internal market and an economic area without frontiers. The White Paper was approved by the Heads of Governments and, after negotiations, led to the enactment of the Single European Act.

Its major innovation was to extend to practically all of its required legislation a system of qualified majority voting in the Council of Ministers. The criteria agreed were that the adoption of general principles of new policies still required unanimous approval, but measures to implement them would be taken by qualified majority voting. The votes are weighted between member states according to their population: France, Germany, Italy and the UK have ten votes each, Spain has eight, Belgium, Greece, the Netherlands and Portugal five each, and Luxembourg two votes. A qualified majority is represented by a minimum of fifty-four votes out of a total of seventy-six.

Legislative powers of the European Parliament were increased. Where the Council acts by qualified majority the Parliament can amend or reject Council decisions. Unanimous agreement in the Council is needed to overrule rejections or amendments submitted by the Parliament. The latter's approval would be required for application for new membership or association agreements with the Community.

Apart from the completion of the single internal market, the Act called for the convergence of economic and monetary policies, strengthening cooperation in research and technological development, improving living and working conditions, promoting economic and social cohesion by reducing disparities between regions with special help to the least favoured ones, advancing health standards, improving the quality of the environment and ensuring a more rational use of natural resources.

The Single European Act marked a major step forward in the process of European integration. It removed the log jam that had built up through the failure of governments to take decisions that were not unanimous. It ended years of stagnation and relative economic decline. The benefits of a single market were estimated, in the medium term, to bring a rise of about 7.5 per cent in GDP and create some six million new jobs. But an integrated market would not endure without the removal of one of the remaining principal barriers, namely the continued existence of separate national currencies and the lack of a clear common voice with outside countries. That is why, additionally, the Act called for progress to economic and monetary union (EMU) and the extension of the Community's responsibilities to foreign policy and security.

THE ROAD TO MAASTRICHT

In response to the SEA's commitment to economic and monetary union, the European Council of Heads of Governments set up a committee under the chairmanship of Commission President

Delors, which included the governors of all the members' central banks. Its detailed recommendations led to the convening of an intergovernmental conference on EMU, which started work in 1990 and completed it for submission to the European Council meeting in Maastricht in December 1991.

In the meantime, the collapse of communism and the disintegration of the Soviet empire led to dramatic changes in the map of Europe. The two parts of Germany were to be reunited. The former Soviet block splintered into independent states, each anxious to convert their command economies into a fully fledged market system, open to trade and investment from the West.

Reunited Germany emerged as Europe's most powerful country with 80 million inhabitants and a GDP larger than that of any of its European neighbours. It was destined to play a dominant role in trade and investment with the countries of the former Soviet block. This raised the question of Germany's continued commitment to the European Community and its ultimate objective of a full economic and political union. Some feared that a powerful and independent Germany would, for the third time this century, threaten economic and political domination of the European continent.

To their credit the Germans themselves were the first to recognise the dangers and resolved to underline Germany's commitment to a united Europe. They wished their country's unification in 1990 to take place within a European framework and thereby ensure that the united Germany would devote itself to the achievement of the political unification of the European Community. Thus, however powerful, Germany would become an integral part of a European Union within which its voice could never be dominant.

To this end German Chancellor Kohl and French President Mitterrand proposed in April 1990 that negotiations for a political union should take place in parallel with the intergovernmental conference on EMU, already agreed. The proposal was accepted by all the Community governments and a second intergovernmental conference, this time for Political Union, was convened at the end of 1990 with the remit to make its recommendations to the same European Council due to meet in December 1991.

EUROPEAN UNION

The recommendations of both intergovernmental conferences became the subject of intense negotiations by the European Council in Maastricht on 9 and 10 December 1991. They resulted in an agreement to conclude a new Treaty on European Union. Though founded on the European Community, parts of it were kept outside the Community's institutional framework. It thus produced a complex and uneven settlement within which some decisions were far-reaching and others represented rather tentative steps towards still undefined goals. This was not entirely surprising, because the two intergovernmental conferences worked separately and their respective proposals remained uncoordinated. However, it was made clear that the Treaty was not the last word on European Union. In its text the Treaty is described as a new stage in the process of creating an ever closer union. It includes a firm commitment to convene a new intergovernmental conference in 1996 to review the Treaty's operation and revise it, where necessary, to fulfil its final objective.

The uneven nature of the Treaty springs also from the fact that EMU, an objective long sought, was well defined by the Delors Committee. It stemmed directly from the SEA and was the logical completion of the internal market by setting out progressive steps to monetary union with a single European currency and fully coordinated economic policies to underpin it. A timetable was agreed for the achievement of EMU, with a single currency replacing national currencies by 1997, if a majority of members complied with the conditions laid down for the transition. Failing that, a single European currency would in any case be established for conforming member states by 1999 at the latest.

Extended and new competences of the Union were agreed within the Community's institutional framework. These dealt with social policy, education, vocational training, youth affairs, public health, cultural issues, consumer protection, trans-European networks in the areas of transport, telecommunications and energy infrastructures, industrial policy including research and technological cooperation, economic and social cohesion, the environment and, finally, cooperation in the development of Third-World countries. Most of these activities were already being pursued by the European Community, but the new

Treaty gave them full legitimation and laid down clear decision-making procedures for each area of Community competence. While unanimity was still retained in the formulation of new policies in some of the competences, legislation implementing the policies would largely be enacted by qualified majority in the Council of Ministers.

The one issue which very nearly led to the collapse of the treaty negotiations covered aspects of social policy. To provide reassurance for labour and the trade unions that the single market would be accompanied by an improvement of working conditions, the Commission introduced the Social Charter, which included aims such as maximum working hours, reasonable incomes and workers' participation in the decisions of their employers affecting their working conditions. The Social Charter was adopted by the European Council in 1989 with Mrs Thatcher, the then British Prime Minister, dissenting. The eleven governments that had approved the Social Charter wanted to incorporate it in the Maastricht Treaty and to subject most of its provisions to majority voting in the Council. Mr Major refused point blank, having given an undertaking to his Conservative backbenchers in Parliament to resist its imposition. In the end a device was found by a protocol to the Treaty embodying the so-called Social Chapter, which excluded Britain from its effect. Community institutions were entrusted with carrying it out, but without British participation.

To secure support for the Treaty from the poorer members of the Community it was agreed to establish a new cohesion fund by the end of 1993, which would provide finance, additional to the existing regional and social funds, to help reduce the economic gap between Europe's regions. The fund would be largely devoted to financing projects in the field of the environment and transport infrastructure.

The part of the Treaty devoted to Political Union is less impressive and commits members to intergovernmental cooperation outside the institutional framework of the existing European Community, though it would grant the European Commission and Parliament the right to be consulted. However, all decisions would stay outside the jurisdiction of the European Court of Justice. Most decisions would be reached by consensus or unanimity, except in the implementation of some policies, agreed unanimously to be subject to qualified majority voting. There is a real danger that this process will perpetuate the kind of virtual stalemate that characterised most decision making in the European Community for some twenty years before the enactment of the SEA.

Nevertheless the Treaty firmly established a common foreign and defence policy. This will include all questions relating to external security of the Union, including the framing of a defence policy which, in terms used in the Treaty 'might, in time, lead to a common defence'. To the latter end Western European Union (WEU), which has nine EC members and which others are invited to join, would become 'the defence component of the Union'.

Another area of new competences within the Treaty, but outside the EC's institutional framework, covers justice and home affairs. These include asylum and immigration from third countries and police cooperation in combating drug addiction, fraud and terrorism. Decisions within this area are, however, firmly based on intergovernmental cooperation and subject to unanimous agreement between governments.

The European Parliament acquires new and extended powers, though still far short of the full democratic control that normally applies in parliamentary democracies. In certain major sectors the Parliament will exercise powers of co-decision with the Council of Ministers, allowing it to reject a proposal if agreement cannot be reached between the two institutions in a joint Conciliation Committee. This procedure applies mainly to policies where qualified majority is provided for Council decisions. It covers all internal market legislation, free movement of people, common policies for research and development, trans-European networks, training, education, culture, health, consumer affairs and the environment programme. Where unanimity in the Council applies or on matters of intergovernmental cooperation the Parliament's role remains merely consultative.

The Parliament's powers of control over the Commission are also strengthened. The appointment of the Commission and its President will be subject to parliamentary approval at the start of their mandate, which, from the beginning of 1995, is to be for five years and timed to coincide with the Parliament's own term of office.

SUBSIDIARITY

All the activities of the Community which do not fall within its exclusive competence will be subject to the principle of subsidiarity. This means that the Community will only take action when its objectives cannot be sufficiently achieved by member states acting separately and when it is considered that these objectives could be better achieved by the Community. Subsidiarity has an even wider meaning in countries with federal structures of government. It requires governmental decisions to be taken at the lowest level possible and closest to the citizen, with the higher tiers of government being able to act only where the common interest so requires.

With the Community implicitly moving towards a federal structure, the principle of subsidiarity will become an increasingly important means of limiting the concentration of powers at European level and, where not absolutely essential, their diffusion down to member states and to regional and local tiers of government. To involve such sub-national units of government in the work of the Community, it was agreed that a consultative Committee of the Regions should be set up. It will be consulted on all issues where specific regional and local interests are involved, and account of its opinions will be taken by the Commission and Council of Ministers.

EUROPEAN CITIZENSHIP

The Treaty establishes citizenship of the Union, which is additional to national citizenship of member states. It enshrines the freedom of movement and establishment for individuals throughout the Union. It extends to all citizens the right to vote and be a candidate in local and European elections in the member states of residence, under the same conditions as nationals of that state. No such rights extend as yet to national elections. When outside the Union, citizens will be entitled to protection by diplomatic and consular authorities of any member state. Citizens will have the right to petition the European Parliament or apply to the Ombudsman, who is to be appointed by the Parliament for this purpose.

RATIFICATION

Ratification of the Maastricht Treaty by member states was envisaged by the end of 1992, so that the Treaty could come into force
at the beginning of 1993. Although all member governments and
large majorities in all national parliaments were strongly in favour
of the Treaty, to the surprise of the whole Community the Danish
electorate rejected the Treaty in a referendum in June 1992. The
majority against the Treaty was minuscule (50.7 per cent against,
49.3 per cent for – a difference of some 48,000 votes).

The decision put the whole process into question as the Treaty,
representing a major amendment of the Treaty of Rome, requires
under the latter's rules ratification by all the twelve member states
before it could come into force. The Lisbon summit meeting at
the end of June 1992 nevertheless decided to proceed with
ratification by the remaining member states, leaving the Danish
government to consider its position and make proposals to its
partners about resolving their own problem of ratification.

In contrast to the Danish vote, a referendum held in Ireland
some two weeks later resulted in a massive 69 per cent in favour
with 31 per cent against. Encouraged by favourable opinion polls
in his own country, French President Mitterrand also decided to
hold a referendum, believing that his own political standing
would be strengthened by a decisive vote in favour. During the
course of the French campaign opposition to the government as
well as widespread criticism of Community policies, often not
related to the Maastricht Treaty, escalated and almost defeated
French ratification. In the end, however, the referendum held on
20 September 1992, approved the Treaty by 51.05 per cent with
48.95 per cent voting against.

The British government – which, before the Danish referendum, had easily obtained large parliamentary majorities on the
principles of the Treaty and on the second reading of the ratification bill – faced a major revolt among its more sceptical
backbench party supporters against proceeding with the bill after
the Danish rejection. Responding, Prime Minister John Major
stalled the parliamentary process on the grounds that there was
no point in proceeding until the Danes had indicated a way out
of the impasse and the French referendum was out of the way.

FINANCIAL CRISIS

With mounting political uncertainties and growing doubts about Maastricht being expressed in other Community countries, stability in financial markets was undermined. Speculative attacks on currencies, with either fixed parities inside the Exchange Rate Mechanism (ERM) of the European Monetary System (EMS) or shadowing it from outside, forced devaluations in Spain and Italy, as well as among some Scandinavian currencies that had been shadowing the German Mark, the strongest component of the ERM. Other countries tried to defend their parities by massive intervention in favour of their currencies in the markets, and by dramatic increases in short-term interest rates.

In the end the speculative attacks proved too much for Britain and Italy, both of whom decided to leave the ERM altogether and allow their currencies to float. The British decision seemed to reinforce its government's own scepticism about Maastricht's main pillar of economic and monetary union with a single currency as its ultimate aim. Indeed, the British government had already negotiated a special protocol, annexed to the Treaty, giving its parliament the option to decide before 1998 whether Britain would adopt a single currency.

Holding the six months' presidency of the Community, Britain did, however, have the responsibility for guiding its affairs towards objectives already agreed, including the completion of the legislation for the Single Market, due to start on 1 January 1993. Its other tasks were to find a way out from the impasse caused by the Danish referendum, to reach agreement on the financing of the Community until the end of the century, and to prepare negotiations with several new candidate countries anxious to join the Community. Urged by his partners at the October Birmingham summit, Mr Major decided to restart the stalled ratification process in his parliament. With the Labour opposition voting against the government on this occasion, he only managed this by a very narrow margin of three votes, and that after an undertaking given to some of the Conservative rebels that the final vote in the House of Commons would not take place before a favourable second Danish referendum.

The Edinburgh summit meeting in December 1992 did resolve most of the issues facing it. Agreement was reached, with Denmark being allowed to opt out of the single currency and all actions of the Union with defence implications. Other minor clarifications of Maastricht decisions were also spelt out to allay Danish fears. The Danes accepted that the opt-outs were temporary, could be reversed by them and would, in any case, be put into the melting pot during the next review of the Treaty in 1996. Agreement was also reached on the financial arrangements which would progressively increase the budget from 1.20 per cent of the Community's gross domestic product (GDP) to 1.27 per cent by 1999. Negotiation for the accession of Austria, Finland and Sweden would start immediately, with Norway following later in 1993. Finally, agreement was reached on the closer definition of the principle of subsidiarity and its application to future Community decisions.

By the end of 1992 ten of the twelve member states had ratified the Maastricht Treaty. On the basis of the special agreement negotiated in Edinburgh, the Danish government held a second referendum on 18 May 1993. On this occasion ratification was approved by 58.6 per cent with 43.2 per cent voting against. Britain followed with its own legislation, completing the whole ratification process rather later than originally planned but by the summer of 1993.

ASSESSING MAASTRICHT

The Treaty represents a compromise between those member states that are committed to a union with a federal goal and others who wish to resist any further surrender of their national sovereignties. Among the latter are Britain and Denmark, with the other ten countries favouring to a greater or lesser extent progress towards a federation.

Surprisingly, the clearest definition of a European federation came from British sources between 1935 and 1940, as described in the next chapter. According to this a European federation of democratic states would be based on the rule of law and governed by a representative government answerable to a two-chamber legislature, one chamber representing voters directly and the other the member states. A federal court of justice would uphold the constitution and all legislation enacted under it. The federal powers would cover trade, currency, defence and sufficient tax-raising powers to pay for federal expenditure. An explicit distribution of powers between the federal and state levels was judged necessary to prevent excessive centralisation and to limit federal responsibilities to those matters where national governments, acting on their own, could not satisfy common objectives. The last concept has now emerged in the Maastricht Treaty as the principle of subsidiarity.

The draft treaty on European Union, first presented to governments in Maastricht, described it 'as a new stage in the process leading gradually to a union with a federal goal'. At British insistence this was changed to 'creating an ever closer union among the peoples of Europe' , using wording that had already been used in the preamble to the Treaty of Rome. To prevent the ever closer union becoming too centralised, its competence to act was qualified by the principle of subsidiarity. To the governments favouring a federal goal the concession seemed purely semantic, and they worked for a commitment to a review of the Treaty in 1996 to strengthen the federal character of the Union. A review of the Treaty was agreed but, at British insistence, the term 'federal' was removed from the text.

If one examines the existing Community, it is clear that its institutions, responsibilities and laws, which take precedence over national legislation, already go a good way towards fulfilling the definition of a federation as envisaged by its pre-war British protagonists. The Maastricht Treaty has moved the process further. Trade is a matter for the Community, especially after the Single European Act. Commitment to economic and monetary union foreshadows a single currency. Its revenue budget to finance Community policies comes from its own independent financial resources, consisting of customs duties, agricultural levies and a fixed percentage of value added tax. Finally there is the decision to move ultimately to a common defence, though for this aspect of the common foreign and security policy there is no timetable fixed. Thus Maastricht provides all the essential ingredients for an eventual federation. But there is still some way to go. The common foreign and security policy is not subject to the Community's institutions and remains a matter of intergovernmental cooperation. The goal of a single European currency is still elusive, subject to the most stringent conditions before member states will be able to adopt it. Some may succeed, others might not for a considerable time. This clearly signals variable speeds of progress towards full economic and monetary union.

Finally, the European Parliament does not yet share all the legislative powers with the Council of Ministers. This leaves the Union with a so-called democratic deficit and continues to deprive the ordinary citizen of the type of direct representation in parliamentary control over the government and its actions which their elected representatives already exercise at national level.

PUBLIC REACTION

Perhaps the most disturbing factor is the public scepticism about the Maastricht Treaty demonstrated during the referenda and revealed in public opinion polls in other countries during the ratification process. These showed a yawning gap in understanding of the purposes of the Treaty as between the politicians and opinion-formers, on one side, and a rather bemused public that had difficulty in comprehending what Maastricht was all about. For instance a lot of the criticisms voiced against the intrusive Brussels bureaucracy dictating choice and imposing uniformity were misdirected. The Commission was blamed for decisions taken by national governments in the Councils of Ministers. The issues under attack were almost exclusively concerned with the implementation of the single market and not with Maastricht. Attacks against the common agricultural policy were equally misplaced, as agriculture is not even mentioned in the Maastricht Treaty. European citizenship was seen by some as a means of depriving people of their national identity. Finally, a lot of the opposition to Maastricht reflected the economic recession and the consequent unpopularity of governments and politicians in general.

The critical reactions demonstrated the need to make the public much more aware of the purposes and become involved in the process of European integration. What is clearly missing is 'glasnost' or more openness about the activities of the Community. Instead of leaving negotiations to diplomats and politicians cobbling up deals behind closed doors, the whole Community decision-making process needs to be exposed to full public scrutiny. The European Parliament must acquire full and effective control over Community legislation and the actions of the executive Commission. There is need to identify the ordinary citizen much more closely with the emerging union. One characteristic of the USA is that its citizens accept and respect their federal institutions because these are part of the constitution, spelling out their individual rights and the way that they are governed. There is no similar sense of identity or pride in belonging to the European Union, which continues to be distant from and often incomprehensible to the ordinary citizen. Remedying this is one of the most urgent tasks which will face the Union after the Maastricht Treaty is ratified.

BEYOND MAASTRICHT

There is a long queue of applicants for membership of the Community, all of whom have declared their acceptance of all the obligations of membership including those spelt out in the Maastricht Treaty. Turkey, Cyprus and Malta applied some time ago and hope to join in the foreseeable future. More immediately, several of the EFTA countries, which have only just concluded an agreement with the Community for a European Economic Area, have decided that full membership is preferable. The EEA gave them full access to the Single Market, but did not allow them to participate in the decision-making process which would affect that market. As a result, Austria, Finland, Norway, Sweden and Switzerland have all applied for full membership, though it is unlikely that Switzerland, after a referendum rejection of the EEA, will pursue its application for the time being. Several of the new democracies emerging from the collapsed Soviet empire have also declared their wish to join. These include the so-called four Visegrad countries: Hungary, Poland, the Czech Republic and Slovakia. Others hopeful to join are Slovenia, Croatia, the three Baltic countries, Romania and Bulgaria, with some of the remaining East European countries that ultimately would not wish to be excluded from the emerging European Union.

If most of the potential candidates were to join by the end of the century or soon after, the Union's membership would more than double. If it is to operate effectively its management will need to undergo further major changes. Although qualified majority voting has, under the Maastricht Treaty, been substantially extended, there are still a number of areas where unanimity continues to apply. Reaching unanimous decisions among twelve countries is difficult and lengthy. Unanimity within a union of twenty or more states is a certain recipe for stagnation and no significant decisions in the common interest are likely to be reached except by compromises at the lowest common denominator. The story of the Community in the next chapter provides several examples of the stagnation which the Community suffered because of the lack of consensus to reach unanimous decisions. Failure to take common decisions in the future could only lead to growing disillusionment and the possible splintering or collapse of the Union itself. Substantial future enlargement will thus make it imperative to change the decision-making procedures to make it work.

This is another major task for the review of the Treaty envisaged for 1996. What is clearly needed is a democratic and intelligible constitution setting out the principles and aims of the European Union, enshrining and guaranteeing the rights of individual citizens, respecting the diversity of its peoples and their traditions, and defining the responsibilities of its federal institutions in accordance with the principle of subsidiarity and laying down a clear system of democratic decision-making.

Chapter 2

The road to union

The dramatic changes in the nature of the world which have taken place since the Second World War have had a particularly profound impact upon relations between states in Europe. Nationalism and demands for democratic self-determination, increasingly articulated after the popular uprising throughout central Europe in 1848, finally found satisfaction with the collapse of the German, Austro-Hungarian, Russian and Ottoman empires as a result of the First World War. President Woodrow Wilson's Fourteen Points, the Versailles Treaty and the Covenant of the League of Nations of 1919 were all concerned with establishing independent and sovereign nation states in their place. It was a proud boast that the new national political frontiers, established by the Treaty, were so drawn that only 3 per cent of the European continent's total population lived under alien rule. Judged by the test of democratic national self-determination, no previous European frontiers had been so satisfactory.

Yet, during the following twenty years, democracy in many European countries gave way to totalitarian regimes sustained by aggressive economic and political nationalism. The League of Nations, meant to regulate relations between sovereign states, lacked effective powers to impose its collective will. It weakened and finally collapsed in the face of fascist and Nazi aggression. The advent of the Second World War finally persuaded European countries to seek a new settlement, which would secure peace and move beyond the classic league of independent states towards a very much more far-reaching economic and political union.

Central to post-war development in Western Europe has been

the contribution of federal ideas. Indeed, t…
European integration has been dominated b…
bate between protagonists of federal solu…
defending increasingly out-dated notions of
eignty. It has also been a debate between pi…
believe that the best way to proceed is to reac…
practical steps, without necessarily defining or e… …ng
their ultimate aim, and the so-called visionaries, who believe that
all action should be guided by progress towards a clear objective.
This chapter gives an account of the debate and the resulting
developments.

UNITY BY CONSENT

European history recounts several attempts to unite the conti-
nent under single rule. In the first and second centuries AD the
Roman Empire included all the territories in North Africa, Asia
Minor and Europe bordering on the Mediterranean Sea, and the
rest of colonised Europe stretching from Britain to the Black Sea.
Emperor Charlemagne ruled in 800 AD over most of western
Christendom. In the sixteenth century, through marriage and by
force of arms, the Holy Roman Emperor Charles V controlled
Europe from Gibraltar to Hungary and from Amsterdam to Sicily.
In 1810 Napoleon's empire extended from Spain to the borders
of the Russian and Ottoman empires. Finally, Hitler by 1942, in
pursuit of his goal of a Greater Germany that would last a thousand years, conquered territory in Europe extending from the
Pyrenees to the outskirts of Leningrad, Moscow and Stalingrad,
and from Norway to Greece. Yet, apart from the Roman Empire,
none of the others endured for long and most of them did not
survive their architects.

Our story, however, is concerned with uniting our continent
by consent of its citizens instead of by conquest – an attempt that,
because of this vital difference, offers the near certainty that it
will endure. Serious considerations of union started this century.
A seminal book, *The Great Illusion* by Norman Angell, first published in 1908, analysed the rivalries between the great powers
and causes of war between them. Translated into many languages,
continuously reprinted with occasional new editions over the
following thirty years, it influenced many who were seeking a
different way of conducting international relations. The nub of

argument, appearing in one of the later editions, was contained in the following passage:

> If, in what is now the United States, there had developed from the original thirteen colonies half-a-dozen independent sovereign nations (as the Spanish American colonies developed into a dozen nations) each with its own army, navy, tariff, currency, they would have fought each other as Bolivia fights Paraguay, Chile and Peru. If Pennsylvania does not fight Ohio, but France does fight Germany, it is not because those who live in Pittsburgh or Toledo are necessarily superior in social morality or intention, or in peacefulness, to those living in Cologne or Lille, but because history has developed a federal bond in the one case, and not in the other. If, by some happy accident of European history some form of federal bond had been left (as a legacy, say, of the Roman Empire) so that we had today a United States of Europe in which France and Germany occupied much the position that Pennsylvania and Ohio occupy in the American system – or if they occupied the position of a French or German Canton in the Swiss Confederation – war would have been as unknown between the two Rhine nations, as it is between States of the American Union.

With the approach of the First World War many attempts were made to promote peace through federal means. Albert Einstein, Lujo Brentano, Prince Lichnovsky and others set up *Neues Vaterland* in Berlin in 1914. Article 1 of its objects was: 'the promotion of all efforts to imbue the policy of the European powers with civilised notions of peaceful competition and supranational unification'. The Union of Democratic Control founded in London in 1914 by Ramsay MacDonald, Charles Trevelyan and Norman Angell issued a Manifesto urging that 'policy should no longer be arrived at through a balance of power but should be directed to establishing a European Federation of States'. A Dutch committee set up in the same year called for Europe to become 'a closely united league of states or a federal state'. Although their voices were not heeded and Europe plunged into the First World War that claimed millions of lives, the ideas were not dead. In 1918, Walther Rathenau, later to be assassinated after he became German Foreign Minister, called for the replacement of 'international anarchy by a voluntarily accepted higher authority'.

LEAGUE OF NATIONS

The Versailles Peace Conference in 1919 chose, however, a different path. The League of Nations, established by the Treaty of Versailles, was created to promote international cooperation and to achieve international peace and security. Membership was not, however, compulsory and the USA never joined it. Germany became a permanent member in 1926, but resigned in 1933 after Hitler came to power. Japan, after being condemned for aggression in China, also resigned in 1933, and Italy followed in 1937 after successfully defying the League over her conquest of Abyssinia, a country that was also a member of the League. The failure of the League of Nations to maintain international peace was largely due to national sovereignty remaining unfettered and from the lack of effective sanctions to secure compliance with League decisions. The existence of the League did, however, for a time, put European unification on the back burner.

In 1923, in a book entitled *Pan-Europa*, Austrian Count Coudenhove-Kalergi argued that the unification of the nations of Europe 'will either come voluntarily through the formation of a European federation or will be forced on Europe by a Russian conquest'. He founded the Pan-Europa Union, which quickly gained a large membership and much public support. At its first congress in Vienna in October 1926, more than 2,000 European politicians, educationists, businessmen, lawyers and journalists demanded the 'political and economic unification of all states from Portugal to Poland' and the progressive development of 'a United States of Europe'.

Elected President of the Pan-Europa Union in 1927, French Foreign Minister Aristide Briand decided to take a major initiative in pursuit of the Union's objective. Addressing the Assembly of the League of Nations in September 1929, Briand proposed a project for the establishment of a European federal union. His detailed memorandum 'On the organisation of a Europe Federal Union' was sent to all European governments in May 1930. The responses received showed, however, complete miscomprehension, especially by those larger powers, for whom the ceding of national sovereignty was inconceivable. Indeed, the emerging world economic crisis of the 1930s stimulated defensive measures of national protection and a growing authoritarianism that, like fascism and national socialism, proclaimed the nation state as the sole arbiter of its destiny. Aggressive designs upon weaker neighbours threatened the international order and made war increasingly likely.

THE FEDERAL ALTERNATIVE

In a public lecture in 1935 Philip Kerr, later to become Lord Lothian, declared that 'war is inherent in an international system based on national sovereignty'. A growing body of intellectuals backed federalism as a solution to the problems of war. In Britain they included Norman Angell, H.N. Brailsford, G.D.H. Cole, Harold Laski, R.H. Tawney and Leonard Woolf. Lionel Robbins, at the beginning of 1939, applied a federalist analysis to the international economic crisis in a series of prestigious lectures delivered in Geneva, which were later published as *The Economic Causes of War.*

Indeed, London became the centre from which the federal idea received a new lease of life. In 1938 a number of young men, deeply concerned at the seemingly inevitable progress towards war, decided to launch a movement in favour of a democratic European organisation with supranational powers that became known as Federal Union. They appealed to several hundred selected personalities in public life for support. Some thirty-five prominent people, including Lionel Curtis, Lord Lothian, Lionel Robbins, Arnold Toynbee, former Times editor Wickham Steed, J.B.Priestley, Vaughan Williams and Barbara Wootton, signed a declaration 'that national sovereignty had to be overcome and that federation must replace it'.

Widely publicised, the declaration gained Federal Union several thousand supporters. At its first national conference of local groups and branches, held in July 1939, it set up a National Council. Considerable interest in the federal idea was stimulated by two influential books published in London at the time. They were *Union Now* by the American Clarence Streit and *The Case for Federal Union* by W.B. Curry. But the movement was too late to avert the war.

After the outbreak of the war considerable thought was given to the development and publication of a series of closely argued tracts on federal themes. Sir William Beveridge, Master of University College, Oxford, chaired the newly established Federal

Union Research Institute. A major intellectual input came from people like Professor Ivor Jennings, Lionel Curtis, Kenneth Wheare, Lionel Robbins, James Meade, Friedrich von Hayek, Harold Wilson, Barbara Wootton and others.

ANGLO-FRENCH UNION

In the autumn of 1939 the concept of a European federation based on Britain and France, to be joined after the war by a democratic Germany, gained in strength. The Foreign Office worked on a scheme for an Anglo-French Union, a project which secured Prime Minister Neville Chamberlain's backing on 1 March 1940. Arnold Toynbee, then at Chatham House, drew up, on the basis of the Foreign Office project, an Act of Perpetual Association between France and Britain which was approved by the Foreign Secretary Lord Halifax and by Sir Alexander Cadogan, his permanent secretary.

In the meantime German troops, after invading Holland and Belgium, advanced into France, where resistance started to crumble. To stop the final collapse, Jean Monnet, an Anglo-French civil servant coordinating Allied war supplies, decided to seize the initiative. He proposed a dramatic declaration by the two governments of the solidarity of British and French interests through the merger of their respective governments into a single cabinet and by uniting their two parliaments. His ideas gained support from some British civil servants and from General de Gaulle. Neville Chamberlain persuaded Winston Churchill, his successor as Premier, to include the project on the cabinet agenda. To Churchill's surprise it received enthusiastic support among his colleagues. As a result, on 16 June 1940, the Cabinet agreed to propose to the French Government that 'France and Britain shall no longer be two nations but one Franco-British Union'.

Paul Reynaud, the French Prime Minister to whom de Gaulle had transmitted the text of the British declaration, recognised that the proposal could avert the collapse of French resistance and argued forcefully its acceptance by his own cabinet colleagues. French defeatism, however, had reached a point of no return. His pleas fell mostly on deaf ears and by the next day he was forced to resign. Marshall Pétain took his place, determined to seek an armistice.

PLANNING FOR PEACE

Although Monnet's initiative failed on this occasion, detailed discussions continued about a post-war organisation of Europe on federal lines. Governments of occupied countries, exiled to Britain, were much involved. An international committee of Federal Union, which included representatives of sixteen European countries, was formed in 1941. By July 1943 they produced two memoranda advocating a European federation.

East European representatives were particularly strongly in favour of union. In 1941 Polish, Czech, Yugoslav and Greek representatives negotiated a Declaration of Solidarity between their governments. General Sikorski, leader of the Polish government in London, favoured the unification of the whole of Europe with a federal union between Poland and Czechoslovakia as a first step. He persuaded President Benes to sign a Czechoslovak–Polish confederal treaty in January 1942. Amongst the west Europeans, Belgian Foreign Minister Paul-Henri Spaak negotiated with his Netherlands and Luxembourg colleagues and, by 1944, they agreed to set up the Benelux Customs Union.

Reflecting these discussions and his own growing commitment to some permanent organisation of post-war Europe, Winston Churchill wrote the following on 21 October 1942 in a minute to his Foreign Secretary: 'Hard as it is to say now, I trust that the European family may act unitedly as one under a Council of Europe. I look forward to a United States of Europe in which the barriers between the nations will be greatly minimised and unrestricted travel will be possible. I hope to see the economy of Europe studied as a whole.'

On 21 March 1943, in a broadcast beamed worldwide, Churchill called for the establishment after the war of a Council of Europe in which both victor and vanquished would participate. As he put it: 'We must try to make the Council of Europe, or whatever it may be called, into a really effective League, with all the strongest forces concerned woven into its texture, with a High Court to adjust disputes, with forces, armed force, national or international or both, held ready to enforce the decisions and prevent renewed aggression and the preparation of future wars.'

The Federal Union tracts and the recommendations of the exiled governments were smuggled into occupied Europe and distributed among resistance movements. Many of the latter developed the ideas further in planning for the post-war world. Some books and pamphlets by the British federalists reached Mussolini's political prisoners confined on the island of Ventotene off Naples. Altiero Spinelli and Ernesto Rossi, two of their leaders, after intensive study of the literature received, issued the Ventotene Manifesto in 1941, which provided the intellectual foundation of the Italian Federalist Movement launched in August 1943. After the liberation, Spinelli and Rossi went to Geneva to organise a meeting of representatives of resistance groups from several countries to work out a common programme. The final Declaration of the conference calling for a European Federation owed much to the ideas worked out by Federal Union.

In the meantime, Jean Monnet, by now with the Free French in Algiers, was also engaged in planning for peace. He wrote: 'There will be no peace in Europe if States reconstitute themselves on a basis of national sovereignty... European countries are too confined to ensure prosperity and essential social developments for their people. It follows that European States should form themselves into a federation or a "European entity" which would make them a joint economic unit.'

As the liberation of the Continent progressed, federalist organisations sprang up in various countries. A conference on European Federation was held in Paris in March 1945. It was opened by the French author, Albert Camus, followed by Spinelli, and was attended by federalists from France, Italy, Switzerland, Austria, Germany, Spain, Greece and Britain, including George Orwell. Dutch, Belgian and German branches of Federal Union were formed soon after. At international meetings held in 1946 at Hertenstein, near Lucerne in Switzerland, in Luxembourg and in Paris it was agreed to found the European Union of Federalists which was to play a central part in the battle for European unification.

Meanwhile Churchill, after his defeat in the 1945 General Election, decided to absent himself from Parliament for a few months and undertake a series of speaking engagements in America and Europe about the state of the world and his vision for the future. In March 1946 he delivered a speech in Fulton, Missouri, in which he first spoke publicly about the division of Europe. As he put it 'From Stettin in the Baltic to Trieste in the

Adriatic, an iron curtain has descended across the Continent.'
Although he did not regard war with Russia as imminent or
inevitable, he argued for a policy of strength and unity in the face
of the Soviet Union and its Central and Eastern European communist satellites.

Speaking in Western Europe, Churchill developed his ideas
about European unity. In November 1945, in Brussels, he first
mentioned the idea of 'the United States of Europe'. In September 1946 he delivered a speech in Zurich that caught the
imagination throughout Europe. In it he spoke of the post-war
distress for which he saw, as a remedy, a partnership between
France and Germany and the building of 'a kind of United States
of Europe'. It was remarkable that so soon after the end of the
war he recognised the crucial importance of Franco-German
reconciliation. Although during the war he appeared to link
Britain fully with the future of Europe, he now appeared more
ambivalent about it. To him the British Empire and Commonwealth came first and the relationship with Europe only in some
form of close but external association.

ECONOMIC CRISIS

At the time, Europe faced the dislocation of the entire fabric of
its economy. Machinery was obsolete or in disrepair, currencies
were discredited and as people despaired social unrest grew. At
the end of the war American Lend–Lease was stopped abruptly.
Loans raised in the USA by individual European countries, intended for investment and future reconstruction, were having to
be spent on raw materials and the immediate consumption of
food and fuel.

The Americans came to realise that if Europe's economy collapsed the US would suffer gravely and that for the sake of
political stability and economic health the Americans had to act.
In June 1947 General Marshall, the American Secretary of State,
offered to provide essential financial and economic help for
European recovery. His offer was conditional on the Europeans
coordinating their needs and acting together in allocating the
aid. The West Europeans responded with alacrity; but although
the offer was extended to the whole of Europe, the Russians
refused the Marshall offer. They dubbed it a programme to
interfere in the internal affairs of other states. Eastern European

countries under Soviet control were instructed to reject the offer. And so the Marshall Plan, without the involvement of communist-controlled Europe, laid the foundation for economic cooperation between democratic states alone. By April 1948, under American pressure, the recipients of the aid agreed to set up the Organisation for European Economic Co-operation, which that took responsibility for coordinating the American aid and liberating intra-European trade.

Following the Soviet rejection of the Marshall Plan, the cold war in Europe grew. In February 1948 a Communist coup took place in Czechoslovakia and a month later Jan Masaryk, Czech Foreign Minister since 1940, son of the country's first President and a strong protagonist of European unity, took his life or, as some suspect, was murdered. In response to the growing threat from the East, the governments of Britain, France, Belgium, the Netherlands and Luxembourg signed a treaty in Brussels establishing a joint defence pact. They did not, however, possess adequate forces on their own and immediately approached the US Government for American involvement. Within eleven months an alliance with the USA and Canada was negotiated and the North Atlantic Treaty Organisation was established.

CONGRESS OF EUROPE

All these events added urgency to the attempts to move from rhetoric to action in uniting Europe. At the initiative of Churchill's son-in-law, Duncan Sandys, the various organisations working for European unity were brought together at the first Congress of Europe in May 1948 in The Hague. Some 750 people, representing almost every European nationality, attended as delegates. There were also observers from the USA and the British Commonwealth and 250 or so members of the world's press. More than fifty of the delegates were former prime ministers, foreign ministers and serving cabinet ministers. Churchill presided as Chairman of the Congress. The political committee was presided over by former French Socialist Prime Minister, Paul Ramadier, the economic committee by former Belgian Premier, Paul Van Zeeland, and the cultural committee by the distinguished Spanish author, Professor Salvador de Madariaga.

Final resolutions of the Congress formed the basis of pressure soon to be exerted on European governments by the principal congress delegates. The political resolution called for a European Union or Federation, to which individual nations would transfer some of their sovereign rights in order to act politically and economically together and to aim at integrating and developing their common resources. Germany would form part of it. A European Assembly, chosen by the Parliaments of the participating nations, was to be urgently convened to advise on the measures needed to achieve the political and economic union of Europe. Membership would be open to all European democracies willing to subscribe to a Charter of Human Rights. A Court of Justice with powers to implement the Charter was to be set up. The economic resolution called for the free movement of people, goods and capital, a customs union and monetary unification. In the cultural field recommendations included the setting up of a European Cultural Centre and the promotion of European education.

Finally, to further the aims of the Congress, it was agreed to found the European Movement as an independent pressure group, with Duncan Sandys as its first international President. Forty-five years after its formation the Movement continues to play the coordinating role in thirty European countries for all voluntary organisations working for European unity.

COUNCIL OF EUROPE

Several political and institutional developments stemmed from the recommendations of the Congress. There was the European Payments Union, the European Cultural Foundation in Amsterdam and the College of Europe in Bruges. But by far the most significant development was an agreement to set up a Consultative Assembly of members of national parliaments and a Committee of Ministers to be known as the Council of Europe. The Statute of the Council of Europe was signed in London on 5 May 1949 – a date which was fixed as the official Europe Day. The signatories were the five Brussels Pact members together with Denmark, Norway, Sweden, Ireland and Italy. Its declared aim was to achieve a closer union between its members in economic, social, scientific, legal and administrative matters. It further concerned itself with the promotion and protection of human rights and fundamental liberties. It adopted the European Convention for the Protection of Human Rights and set up the European

Court, whose judgments were to be binding on member states.

At its first meeting in August 1949 the Assembly elected former Belgian Premier and Foreign Minister Paul-Henri Spaak as its President. At the end of the first session he declared: 'I came to Strasbourg convinced of the need for a United States of Europe. I leave with the certainty that union is possible.' The Council of Europe was the first European political organisation. Its Assembly members, appointed by national parliaments, sat in the Chamber in alphabetical order and not in national delegations, and voted as individuals. Yet it became a place of disappointed hopes. It never acquired legislative powers. The Committee of Ministers could only make recommendations to member governments and these in practice required unanimous agreement, so that there could be no agreement if any one minister objected. It is hardly surprising, therefore, that the Council was unable to fulfil the hopes of the Hague Congress for a political union. Within two years of taking office, Spaak resigned disillusioned. As he put it later: 'of all the international bodies I have known, I have never found any more timorous or more impotent'.

INTEGRATION ON FEDERAL LINES

Meanwhile, world events gave ever more urgency to the need for European unity. The Berlin blockade by the Russians started in August 1948. A year later the Soviet Union admitted that it possessed the atomic bomb. At about the same time the newly elected German Chancellor, Konrad Adenauer, announced that the Federal Republic wished to join not only the Council of Europe but also the Atlantic Alliance. German industrial reconstruction was also making remarkable progress. French alarm at the re-establishment of a major industrial and possibly military power on its borders urgently concentrated the minds of French leaders. Jean Monnet saw his opportunity to subsume the German problem. He submitted to the French Government a proposal 'to place the whole of Franco-German coal and steel production under a common High Authority, in an organisation open to the participation of the other countries of Europe.' While Germany would once again be treated as an equal, the pooling of basic resources would make war between France and Germany 'not only unthinkable but materially impossible.'

The French Government approved the plan and Foreign

Minister Robert Schuman, in a declaration made public on 9 May 1950, proposed the creation of the European Coal and Steel Community to establish a common basis for economic development and as a first step in the federation of Europe. The common High Authority would become a European power independent of the member states in the fields entrusted to it. Schuman made this principle of supranationality a prior condition for negotiations on a treaty to set up the Community. Six countries declared their acceptance of the proposal, namely France, Germany, Italy and the three Benelux countries. Britain's Labour Government, which had only recently and with difficulty nationalised its coal and steel industries, was unwilling to cede control of them to a supranational organisation and declined the invitation.

The Treaty of Paris, setting up the ECSC, was signed on 18 April 1951. In addition to the independent supranational High Authority, the Treaty provided for a Common Assembly, composed of national parliamentarians, to exercise democratic control over the executive, and a Court of Justice to resolve disputes and whose decisions were binding on the members. The recommendations of the High Authority had to be approved by a special Council of Ministers representing the member states. Some of their decisions, according to the treaty, were taken by qualified majority, others by unanimous agreement.

Now the question arose of how to move from a sectoral authority to a genuine political power with much wider jurisdiction. Proposals were soon made for supranational authorities in other fields such as transport, public health and agriculture, but these did not receive much support from member governments.

DEFENCE

Added urgency for further European integration came following the outbreak of the Korean war in June 1950. The North Koreans, fully armed and backed by the Russians, seemed to provide a dress rehearsal for what might soon happen in Europe. Soviet troops and those of its satellites heavily outnumbered allied forces in Europe. The Americans were fighting in Korea, the French in Indo-China and British troops were scattered all over the world. Only Germany could make a significant contribution to common defence. Yet the re-armament of Germany was very difficult for the French to swallow. Jean Monnet urged once again 'to integrate

Germany into Europe by means of a broader Schuman Plan, taking the necessary decisions within a European framework'. He persuaded the new French Premier, René Pleven, to present his plan to the French National Assembly. He proposed 'the creation, for common defence, of a European Army under the authority of the political institutions of a united Europe'. The Assembly approved the plan and for a brief period it seemed that a United States of Europe would be achieved.

Negotiations started in February 1951 with all European members of NATO invited to participate. While Britain, hostile to federalist objectives, once again refused to take part, a Treaty establishing a European Defence Community was negotiated and signed between the six ECSC members in May 1952. Yet the creation of the EDC posed the problem of adequate democratic and political control. It was realised that a political authority was an essential accompaniment to a European army. A special article was therefore included in the EDC Treaty for a democratic assembly to exercise such control. The Assembly of the Coal and Steel Community was to be entrusted with drafting a Treaty constituting a European Political Authority.

By 1954, however, difficulties arose over the ratification of the Defence Community Treaty. After the fall of several French governments and Britain's refusal to join the EDC, circumstances were changing. The death of Stalin promised a possible lessening of the cold war and the need to build a European army became less urgent. Although France has been the strongest protagonist of supranational institutions, the new French Government of Pierre Mendès-France was lukewarm. Opponents of federal solutions and protagonists of French independence and national sovereignty were gaining the upper hand. In August 1954 Mendès-France presented the EDC Treaty for ratification in a noncommittal speech and the French National Assembly failed to approve it. Thus the EDC was killed, as was the proposal for a European Political Community. As one consequence, Germany soon became a full member of the Atlantic Alliance.

After the collapse of the EDC there was fear among supporters of European unification that the partially supranational ECSC might also be swept away. European leaders such as Spaak, Monnet, Adenauer, and the Dutch Foreign Minister Johan Beyen feared that time was against them unless unification was given a new impulse. Two factors were clear. There was no chance of creating a federal state in the immediate future. It was, however, becoming increasingly obvious that no individual West European state would on its own be able to solve its economic problems.

ECONOMIC COMMUNITY

Monnet favoured another sectoral step forward. He wanted nuclear power and its development for peaceful purposes to be added to the responsibilities of the Coal and Steel Community. The Benelux countries and the Germans on the other hand favoured the creation of a customs union. To persuade the French to take part in discussions on wider economic issues, the others decided to support Monnet's proposals on atomic energy. A conference of foreign ministers was convened at Messina in June 1955. At the end of difficult negotiations agreement was reached to create two new organisations, one an atomic community and another for a common market. Spaak, with a small group of experts, was entrusted with drawing up a plan of action. His report, delivered in 1956, became the guiding document for the intergovernmental negotiations that started in June of that year.

The failure of the Anglo-French Suez adventure had a traumatic effect on the French. They realised that their days as a world power were over. And so, when discussions were held in the French National Assembly in January 1957, general approval was voiced in favour of closer cooperation with the other European states, Indeed the weak economic position of the country left them little alternative but to go along with proposals to join an economic community. By February negotiations were completed. France was to enter the common market together with her overseas dependencies and the ownership of fissile materials was to be vested in Euratom. The Treaties were signed in Rome on 25 March 1957.

The EEC Treaty was separate from that of the Coal and Steel Community, but the institutional framework was similar, with a Council of Ministers retaining ultimate control over decisions and legislation, and a Commission acting as the executive organ guiding the Community towards its Treaty objectives. A Court of Justice would adjudicate and a parliamentary Assembly, in due course to be directly elected, would have a largely consultative role. The Treaty thus contained both intergovernmental and supranational elements. Some decisions were subject to qualified majority voting; others, particularly in adopting new responsibilities or policies, required unanimous agreement. Progress towards full federation was not spelt out but neither was it excluded. It all depended on the political will of member states.

Invited, Britain sent a civil servant as an observer to the Messina conference, but it did not accept the Messina resolution. When the negotiations progressed towards the creation of a customs union, Britain decided to withdraw, doubting whether, as in the case of the EDC, anything would come of them. When the Treaty was actually signed and soon afterwards ratified by all of its six members, alarm bells started ringing in Westminster. If the Common Market of the Six was becoming a reality, Britain faced economic isolation from the Continent and had to rethink its strategy. Britain proposed an industrial free trade area that excluded agriculture. To strengthen her bargaining power, Britain formed the European Free Trade Area, with six other European countries that did not belong to the EEC, with the object of merging EFTA and the EEC into a wider free trade area. The proposal was, however, doomed from the start because it ignored the commitment of the Six to the Economic Community, including agriculture, which they conceived as another major step towards further political integration. Britain's approach was rebuffed because the Six, and France in particular, were not prepared to water down their existing arrangements or abandon ultimate union.

GAULLIST BRAKE ON PROGRESS

When General de Gaulle came to power in France in 1958, progress towards the federation of Europe faced a new obstacle. Although de Gaulle was in favour of closer European political cooperation, he was critical of the EC method with its supranational elements. These he wanted to subordinate to inter-governmental political control. He was hostile to the ECSC and Euratom and was showing concern about the growing authority of the EC Commission. He opposed direct elections to the parliamentary Assembly and wanted the existing Communities capped with an inter-state political organisation, in which individual national sovereignty would be preserved by the unanimity rule. While France's partners were ready to talk about political cooperation in fields not covered by the existing Communities, none of them was willing to give up the supranational elements.

Following a conference of the six Heads of State in Paris early in 1961, a preparatory working committee was set up under a French chairman Christian Fouchet. During the same year Britain applied for full membership of the EC. The Benelux governments and Italy were willing to discuss political co-operation, provided that nothing would affect the status of NATO or the British desire to join the Community. As the subsequent negotiations were to show, there was no ultimate meeting of minds. De Gaulle wanted a 'Europe of the States' with no supra-nationality in politics or economics and a European Europe with its own distinctive foreign and defence policy guided by France. The others, and in particular the Dutch, wanted full economic integration and no political union without Britain, which was seen as the guarantor of Europe's commitment to the Atlantic Alliance. As a result the various proposals from the Fouchet Committee failed, and political union disappeared from the European agenda throughout the remainder of General de Gaulle's Presidency of France.

Indeed, de Gaulle's reaction showed a growing hostility to the European Community and its further enlargement and development. When Britain was rebuffed over her proposal for a wider free trade area, the British Premier Harold Macmillan decided to seek full membership of the EC in 1961. Ireland, Denmark and Norway applied alongside. The British negotiations were conducted by Edward Heath and seemed close to success when, in January 1963, de Gaulle used the occasion of Macmillan's decision to acquire the American Polaris missiles to declare a French veto on British entry.

Although initially there was bad feeling about the veto among France's partners, the Community continued to develop, with major decisions being taken on the common agricultural policy. Yet there was a growing divergence between the federalist and Gaullist positions. On 1 January 1966 the major exceptions to the use of majority voting, allowed during the first eight transitional years of the Treaty, were to come to an end, so that theoretically an individual country could be outvoted. The completion of the industrial customs union and the agricultural common market were planned for mid-1967. A single external tariff and agreement to transfer income from agricultural levies to the Community was the starting point for a federal budget. The

Dutch would not agree to this unless the budget became subject to more effective democratic accountability by strengthening the budgetary powers of the European Parliament. In response to this view the European Commission submitted a package proposal for direct revenues for the Community and for an effective budgetary vote for the European Parliament.

The French wanted the proposed financial regulation, which would pay for the agricultural policy, but refused any increase in the Parliament's powers. At the Council of Ministers in June 1965 no agreement was reached and France decided to boycott the Community's decision-making mechanism, in direct breach of her Treaty obligations. The other five continued to meet, while the French chair remained empty. In September de Gaulle called for a revision of the treaties. He refused to accept majority voting, which was due to come into force in 1966, as it would deprive France of her sovereignty. The five were not prepared to yield. Indeed, as majority voting was to come in on 1 January, subsequent French absence would not stop the others from taking decisions on their own.

Pressures in France, however, began to tell. The farmers and industrial and financial circles feared the economic consequences of the boycott, let alone a break with the Community. In the December 1965 French presidential elections the candidates of the centre, Jean Lecanuet, and of the socialists, François Mitterrand, strongly criticised the French Government's position. Indeed Lecanuet called for rapid progress towards a federal political union with direct elections to the European Parliament. His unforeseen high vote of 17 per cent forced de Gaulle into a second round in which he faced Mitterrand, who also took a strong pro-European stance, echoing Lecanuet's demand for a directly elected European Parliament.

The attack on the Community was clearly unpopular and the government decided to cut its losses and return to the Community's negotiating table on the best possible terms. The basic French demand, presented at the Council meeting in Luxembourg early in 1966, was that majority voting was not to be used where a 'vital national interest' was at stake. As each state would be free to define its own vital national interest, the effect would be that the Community would abandon its supranational features and all decisions would be subject to unanimous agreement. The other five refused to accept this change. In the end they agreed that, where very important national interests were at stake for one or more countries, every attempt should be made to achieve unanimity. The French wanted to add that negotiations should continue until unanimity was reached, but the five others disagreed. The so-called Luxembourg compromise was in effect an agreement to disagree. The Treaty was left intact, but in practice no major decisions were taken without unanimous agreement.

There followed a period of relative stagnation. The dismantling of customs barriers and the liberalisation of internal trade in industrial goods continued – indeed the customs union was achieved in July 1968, eighteen months ahead of schedule – but no new policies emerged. Although the timetables were adhered to, the Community marked time on further integration or development. Britain's second attempt to join in 1967 was vetoed by de Gaulle within six months of the application. It became increasingly clear that as long as de Gaulle remained at the head of the French Government further progress within the Community would be blocked.

END OF STAGNATION AND ENLARGEMENT

The break came with de Gaulle's resignation in April 1969, following the defeat of his proposals for regional devolution in France that had been submitted to a national referendum. At the Hague Summit meeting in December 1969 French President Pompidou, who succeeded de Gaulle, negotiated financial arrangements for the agricultural policy in which national contributions were replaced by the Community's own financial resources and it was agreed to open negotiations for British entry. The meeting also considered ways in which progress could be made to full Economic and Monetary Union, and the task was entrusted to an ad hoc group, chaired by Luxembourg's Prime Minister, Pierre Werner. The Foreign Ministers were also instructed to submit proposals for political unification by the following July. The final declaration of the Summit, announcing that 'The Community has today arrived at a turning point in its history', clearly marked the resumption of progress.

Following the Summit, negotiations settled the system of the Community's own financial resources, through the payment to the Community of all agricultural levies and customs duties and up to 1 per cent of the receipts from value added tax. This decision was accompanied by a new Treaty of Luxembourg, which in part transferred national parliamentary control of national contributions to the European Parliament by strengthening its budgetary powers.

Negotiations for the admission of Britain, Ireland, Denmark and Norway started in June 1970 and were successfully concluded by the Summer of 1971. The British House of Commons approved the terms of membership by a majority of 112, aided by the fact that 69 Labour MPs defied their party and joined most of the Conservatives in voting in favour.

In Denmark and Ireland there were large referenda majorities in favour. Only in Norway was membership rejected by a narrow referendum majority. After parliamentary ratification by the applicant countries and the Six, Britain, Denmark and Ireland joined the Community in January 1973.

ECONOMIC AND MONETARY UNION

In the meantime, consideration was given to the Werner Report on Economic and Monetary Union (EC Commission 1970a). The Report recommended a decision-making centre for monetary policy, a Community system of central banks and supervision by the European Parliament. Integration would proceed by stages, in the first of which monetary fluctuations between Community currencies were to be limited through coordinated interventions. The Council of Ministers, meeting in February 1971, did not accept the institutional proposals, though it did agree to increase coordination of economic policies between members, to strengthen cooperation between central banks and to establish methods for providing medium-term financial help. In the monetary field it was agreed that the maximum permitted fluctuation margins between members' currencies would be limited to 2.25 per cent.

This last proposal was popularly known as the 'snake in the tunnel', the tunnel being the agreement to reduce fluctuations against the US Dollar to 4.5 per cent. The snake was finally agreed by the Central banks in April 1974, but it soon collapsed. Following the oil crisis and the massive rise in the cost of primary products, major monetary instability and inflation threatened the agreements reached. In June 1974 Britain, Denmark and Ireland left the snake, and pressures on the economies of the other member states soon rendered all progress towards the Werner Report's version of monetary and economic union politically no longer practicable.

TOWARDS UNION

Much better progress, however, was achieved in the field of political cooperation, called for by the 1969 Summit. Foreign Ministers were instructed to 'study the best way of achieving progress in the matter of political unification, within the context of enlargement'. After relatively speedy negotiations, Community Foreign Ministers adopted, in October 1970, the Davignon Report prepared by the political director of the Belgian Foreign Ministry (EC Commission 1970b). The essence of his report was that harmonisation of foreign policy was the first step towards political union. Its recommendations were that inter-governmental cooperation should start outside the Community framework, through regular exchange of information between foreign ministries, aimed at promoting the harmonisation of views and, where possible, instigating common action. During the years that followed, voluntary political cooperation was strengthened through the adoption of common positions and the coordination of diplomatic action in all international affairs affecting the interests of the European Community. Proposals to establish a permanent secretariat for political cooperation were not, however, accepted because some members were not prepared to see an institutional development outside the framework of the European Community.

Successful progress towards enlargement, economic and monetary union and political cooperation had, by the autumn of 1972, persuaded the Heads of Governments, meeting in Paris, to chart an even more ambitious programme, accompanied by a series of deadlines. These included setting up a European Monetary Cooperation Fund to prepare for full Economic and Monetary Union by 1980. A Regional Development Fund was to be established, as well as a series of action programmes for the protection of the environment, social policy and science and technology. In conclusion, the Heads of Governments declared their intention 'to transform the whole complex of their relations into a European Union by the end of the present decade'. To ensure progress towards it, the leaders asked the Community institutions to draw up a report on the issue before the end of 1975 for submission to another summit conference.

The failure of the Economic and Monetary Union after the world oil crisis persuaded Community governments to make a new attempt to revive progress towards unity. At the Paris Summit of December 1974 three significant decisions were taken. First, to proceed to direct elections of the European Parliament. Then, to institutionalise summit meetings by creating the European Council of Heads of Governments, meeting three times a year. Finally, they asked the Belgian Prime Minister, Leo Tindemans, to draw up a report on the concept and shape of European Union. The importance of these decisions lay in the democratisation of the Community and the creation of the European Council to determine the direction of Community development and resolve conflicts that impeded progress.

The Tindemans Report (EC Commission 1976), submitted in January 1976, took account of the generally lukewarm climate towards major change among member governments at a stage when they were facing a continuing world economic crisis. It identified the main aspects of the proposed union as presenting a united front to the outside world. It recognised that economic interdependence of member states required common policies. which included regional and social responsibilities, to ensure solidarity between them. It called for the development of a greater public awareness of Europe and the enhancement of the authority, effectiveness and legitimacy of the Community's institutions. It did not, however, lay down any detailed plan to be carried out in stages, as did the original Spaak report that led to the setting up of the EEC and Euratom. It was hardly surprising, therefore, that the report had very little effect on the decisions of member governments. The only practical outcome was an invitation to the Council and the Commission to submit annual reports on progress towards the vaguely defined European Union.

The grand design to achieve European Union by 1980 came to nothing. There were only two significant developments that took place before the end of the decade. One was the agreement at the December 1975 Summit to organise the first direct elections to the European Parliament in 1978. By September 1976 agreement on the composition of the Parliament and details of the electoral law were adopted by the Council of Ministers. Owing to delays in the ratification of the electoral law by the national parliaments, the elections had to be postponed to June 1979. The powers of the elected Parliament remained unchanged from that of its nominated predecessor. Apart from its power to approve the Community budget, its only sanction lay in the right to censure the Commission. Its legislative functions were largely consultative. It was clear that the battle for more powers lay ahead.

EUROPEAN MONETARY SYSTEM

The other development arose from a desire to find another way towards economic and monetary unification, following the failure of the Werner Plan. The European monetary snake had lost most of its original participants and by 1979 only five members remained part of it, namely Germany, Denmark and the Benelux countries. In a speech in October 1977 President of the European Commission Roy Jenkins proposed the establishment of a new monetary system. The object was to create a zone of monetary stability in the Community and establish closer financial cooperation. During the subsequent negotiations, spread over four Summits from April 1978 to March 1979, comprehensive agreement was negotiated, bringing the European Monetary System into being. It established the European Currency Unit (Ecu), its value based on a basket of currencies of member states, as a credit reserve and a means of settlement of official debts among Community institutions. Increasingly, its use has extended to the private sector. It operates an exchange rate mechanism (ERM), within which a central rate for the Ecu is fixed for each participating currency. Permitted fluctuations between most currencies are limited, as in the snake, to 2.25 per cent (Italy's permitted fluctuations are within 6 per cent), with a requirement for national central banks to intervene to maintain the levels. Any devaluation or revaluation of individual currencies can only be fixed jointly by all the participating states.

GENSCHER–COLOMBO

The next attempt to restart the process of integration was taken on the initiative of the German and Italian Foreign Ministers

Genscher and Colombo, in 1981 (EC Commission 1981). Greece had entered the Community at the beginning of the year and negotiations for the admission of Spain and Portugal were proceeding. There was a growing feeling that, unless the Community was to be further diluted through enlargement, the decision-making process needed to be strengthened. With economic divergences between member states widening, there was a shared sense of urgency to re-examine the state of the Community and its development.

The proposals were directed at the strengthening of Community institutions and extending their competence to foreign policy, security and cultural affairs. After a year or so of negotiations the Genscher–Colombo Plan was watered down to a solemn declaration issued at the Stuttgart Summit meeting of the Heads of Governments in 1983. This 'reaffirmed their will to transform the whole complex of relations between their States into a European Union'. Without going into specifics, they agreed to the development of a European social policy that, as they said, 'implies in particular the transfer of resources to less prosperous regions; to the strengthening of European Political Cooperation aimed at speaking with a single voice in foreign policy, including political aspects of security; and to the promotion of closer cooperation in cultural matters'. Progress towards these objectives was to be reviewed within five years. Like so many previous declarations, it did not, however, advance its objectives, nor did it clarify the concept of European Union.

THE DRAFT TREATY

The latter task was undertaken within the first directly elected Parliament. In July 1980 Altiero Spinelli founded the 'Crocodile Club', named after a Strasbourg restaurant where supporters of Community reform first met. They formulated a resolution calling on the European Parliament to draw up proposals for institutional reform. In July 1981 the Parliament agreed to the setting up of an Institutional Committee, which would have the task of producing a comprehensive draft treaty for the establishment of a European Union. Spinelli was made the Committee's coordinating rapporteur, with six other rapporteurs undertaking the drafting of separate aspects of the proposals. After nearly three years' work, the draft treaty was adopted on 14 February

1984 by a large majority representing members from all Community countries and from all political party groups. Out of 311 members present, 237 voted in favour, 31 against and 43 abstained.

The Draft Treaty was comprehensive. It placed within the Union all aspects of policy of concern to the existing Community, as well as foreign affairs, defence, education, research and cultural matters. In the allocation of responsibilities to the European institutions, it adopted the so-called principle of subsidiarity. This means that the union 'shall only act to carry out those tasks which may be undertaken more effectively in common than by the Member States acting separately'. The areas of competence are divided into two parts – common action and cooperation between states. Common action would normally be taken by majority voting, whereas cooperation would require unanimous agreement.

Exclusive competence was allocated to the Union for all matters concerning the free movement of people, goods, services and capital, trade and competition policy and, after a transitional period, development aid policy. There would be shared competences, with majority voting, in the fields of economic and monetary affairs, as well as in all other sectoral spheres such as agriculture, social, regional, industrial, environmental, educational and cultural policies. Issues reserved to inter-governmental cooperation were foreign and defence policies.

The institutional arrangements of the Draft Treaty were largely based on the existing Community pattern, but a process of co-decision between the Council of Ministers and Parliament would give equal weight to both. In its provisions the Draft Treaty provided for developments of existing Community responsibilities to achieve an efficient and democratically controlled European Union. It furthermore empowered the European Council, by unanimous agreement, to move further towards a full federation, including the transfer of national armed forces to the Union.

After a wide-ranging public campaign in support of the Draft Treaty, President Mitterrand promised the Parliament, during the French presidency of the Council, to examine and support the draft 'with the basic premise to which we agree'. At the Summit held in Fontainebleau in June 1984, Mitterrand persuaded his fellow Heads of Governments to set up an ad hoc committee of their representatives to examine the Draft Treaty and work out proposals for institutional reform. That committee reported a year later to the Milan Summit, which decided to convene an Intergovernmental Conference to negotiate amendments to the existing treaties as well as a treaty on political cooperation.

THE SINGLE EUROPEAN ACT

The Intergovernmental Conference culminated with a Summit Meeting in Luxembourg at the end of 1985. This negotiated the Single European Act (EC Commission 1986), the first major amendment to the Treaty of Rome, which after ratification came into force in 1987. While the Act's primary objective was the creation by the end of 1992 of a unified Internal Market, it also dealt with a number of recommendations made by the European Parliament in its Draft Treaty for European Union. Explicitly, it committed its signatories to progress towards an economic and monetary union. It also envisaged a common foreign policy and the economic aspects of security. Its institutional amendments were, however, the most far-reaching since the adoption in 1966 of the so-called Luxembourg compromise on decision-making procedures. The latter had virtually precluded the use of qualified majority voting whenever, on an issue, a vital national interest was declared by a member state, with the result that no major decisions were taken without unanimous agreement.

The Single European Act changed the practice. Explicitly, most Council decisions leading to the implementation of the Internal Market were to be taken by qualified majority. Where the Council acted by majority the European Parliament acquired new legislative powers of co-decision. This meant that the Parliament could amend or reject Council decisions. Unanimous agreement in the Council was now needed to overrule rejections or amendments of legislation submitted by the Parliament. Parliamentary approval was also now needed for the admission of new members into the Community and for association agreements with third countries.

The effect of these institutional changes were immediate and dramatic. With nearly 300 legislative measures needing to be agreed between 1987 and the completion of the Single Market by the end of 1992, it would have been impossible to enact them on the basis of consensus or unanimity that used to apply prior to the Single European Act. To illustrate the point, it took seventeen years, under the Rome Treaty's provisions for the right of establishment, before a proposal to enable architects to practice throughout the Community was finally passed under the Single Act in 1988. With majority voting as the rule, the desire not to be defeated in the Council wonderfully concentrated the minds of the ministers trying to reach agreement. Where such consensus did not emerge, the chairman only needed a favourable opinion on the proposed legislation, expressed by a qualified majority of the states, to declare the measure adopted without any further voting. At the same time the European Parliament's increased legislative powers gave it a much greater sense of purpose and responsibility. It worked much more closely with the Commission in examining the legislation and, because of its increased influence, it became the object of much greater attention by interest groups who wished to lobby the legislators.

EUROPEAN UNION

As described in Chapter 1, the provisions of the SEA, which covered issues beyond the completion of the Internal Market, led to the convening of two Intergovernmental Conferences, one on EMU and the other on Political Union. The recommendations resulted in the Maastricht Treaty, which was signed in February 1992 and which, after notable hesitations, was brought to the point of its ratification by all the twelve member states in 1993.

The Single European Act and the Maastricht Treaty together appear to implement most of the recommendations of the European Parliament's 1984 Draft Treaty for European Union, which was born out of Altiero Spinelli's initiative. They laid a genuine foundation for the United States of Europe, advocated by Winston Churchill nearly half a century previously and which seems increasingly likely to become reality by the end of the twentieth century.

Chapter 3

Economic and monetary union

The economic lesson of this century has been that free trade and open markets are a much better recipe for growth and prosperity than are national protection and restrictions. The rapid economic growth of the original six member countries of the Community during its first fifteen years, when customs duties and trading barriers were being removed, was a dramatic demonstration of the liberating and dynamic effects of open markets. One of the main aims of the Single European Act was to repeat this experience.

But there is a danger in the belief that removing barriers to trade is all that is required. 'The market knows best' is a currently fashionable view in some Community countries. So is the view that the less government the better. It is true that national deregulation was required in implementing the Single European Act wherever this conflicted with the objectives of creating a fully integrated European market. This does not, however, mean that market forces need not be regulated and controlled to ensure free and fair competition. The removal of barriers to trade is necessary but that is not all that is needed to achieve a fully integrated market.

Indeed, collective policies complementing free access to the common market are an essential part of the process of integration. The common market is not an end in itself but, as stated in the Treaty setting up the EEC, a means of promoting a continuous and balanced expansion and rapidly rising living standards. If a dynamic and competitive European economy is to be achieved then the Community needs to go beyond a free trade area. That means a common monetary policy leading to a full monetary union. It involves stable and coordinated macro-

economic policies, including a growing approximation of taxation. The market needs a vigorous competition and mergers
policy that promotes efficiency. It needs a common industrial
policy with particular emphasis on research and development of
the new technologies. Finally, the Community's external commercial policy must avoid unjustified protectionism and give a
lead to the achievement of freer international trade.

By far the most important contribution to creating a stable,
dynamic and fully integrated market will be macro-economic
convergence and exchange-rate stability. That is why achieving a
full economic and monetary union has been on the Community's
agenda for some twenty years. The Maastricht Treaty has finally
spelt it out in detail and set a clear timetable for its achievement.

ECONOMIC CONVERGENCE

The Maastricht Treaty has explicitly provided that, in accordance
with the timetable set, an economic policy based on the close
coordination of members' own economic policies is to be
adopted. This is to be based on a principle of an open market
economy with free competition and an efficient allocation of
resources. The coordination will be the responsibility of the
European Commission reporting to the Council of Ministers who,
in their turn, will submit recommendations to the European
Council (consisting of heads of governments) about laying down
the broad guidelines of economic policies of both the member
states and the Community.

The Council will then supervise the process. Where a member
state fails to conform to the guidelines laid down and thus puts
at risk the proper functioning of the economic and monetary
union, the Council, by a qualified majority vote, will require the
defaulting state to correct its policies. This is particularly relevant
to compliance with budgetary discipline based on two criteria.
The first concerns the ratio of planned or actual government
deficit to the gross domestic product (GDP), which should not
exceed 3 per cent. The second aims to reduce the ratio of
government debt to GDP to not more than 60 per cent. Sanctions
to enforce compliance include making public the recommendations to a member state, inviting the European Investment Bank
to reconsider its lending policy to that state, requiring the state
to make an appropriate non-interest bearing deposit with the

Community until the deficit has been corrected and, as a final sanction, imposing fines on the defaulting member.

MONETARY POLICY

Economic convergence cannot, however, be achieved with floating exchange rates. Earlier, the floating of currencies was welcomed by some countries as an automatic means of dealing with balance of payments problems. It was furthermore believed that it would allow each country greater autonomy in the conduct of its economic policies and, by devaluing, improve its competitiveness. In the event, floating currencies have encouraged much more erratic flows of capital, stimulated inflation and impeded growth.

Following the breakdown in the 1970s of the fixed exchange rate system, established by the 1944 Bretton Woods Agreement, the Community has made two attempts to regulate European currencies. The first attempt, in 1972, following up the Werner proposals for monetary union, failed after the world economic crisis in 1973, generated by the explosion of primary commodity prices.

The European Monetary System, set up in 1979, was a much more ambitious project. It established a common currency unit, the Ecu, to which currencies were linked by a central rate within an exchange rate mechanism (ERM). Currencies were allowed to fluctuate within ±2.25 per cent of their central rate (±6 per cent in the case of the £ sterling and the Italian lira). The rates could be 're-aligned', if necessary, but this can only be done by mutual agreement between participating countries. To help individual currencies to stay within the band, all the central banks are obliged to intervene in the foreign exchange markets. Short-term credit support is also available for countries in difficulties.

The Ecu is used for transactions by all Community institutions including the European Investment Bank. By law the Ecu now has the status of a foreign currency in member countries' markets. The private sector has made increasing use of it because of its greater relative stability compared with the individual currencies which form part of it. It is used for bond issues, bank deposits, credit cards, travellers cheques and, increasingly, as a currency for invoicing and for payments. The substantial increase in Ecu exchange transactions, both spot and forward, has also developed its use in international transactions outside the Community. It is now the third most important currency in the international eurobond markets, behind only the dollar and the deutschmark.

A major benefit of the monetary stability brought about by the EMS has been a reduction of the average level of inflation in Europe and a convergence of the economic policies of member states. These have recognised that there is no permanent gain in depreciating the value of their own currency. The most dramatic example of this was the switch in economic policy of the French socialist government which, between 1981 and 1983, pursued a policy of reflation on its own. This led to several damaging devaluations of the French franc and, as a result, a decision to change course. Since 1983 policies pursued in all member countries of the monetary system have followed closely those of West Germany and, as a result, their inflation rates have since converged round the levels traditionally experienced in the Federal Republic. More recently, the high cost of German unification led to higher interest rates to prevent rising inflation. Germany's high rates forced other ERM countries to follow suit and played an important part in the financial crisis in the autumn of 1992. The growing economic recession in the Community brought interest rates down once again and re-established greater stability.

In spite of the greater stability in exchange rates achieved by the monetary system, there are many remaining disadvantages in keeping twelve separate currencies in a market that has now lost its internal frontiers. A telling example of the cost to individuals of the existence of separate currencies when travelling around the Community was provided in 1987 by Mr Ben Patterson, a member of the European Parliament. Starting with £100, he 'changed' his money in telephone transactions with each of the twelve Community countries successively, ending up with only £55.50, or just over half of the original sum. The exercise done by Mr. Patterson is set out in the Table 3.1.

Indeed, the use of twelve different currencies within the present Community is a clear obstacle to a unified market. Investors and traders do not know what one currency will be worth in terms of another. Individual travellers, as illustrated in Table 3.1, have to pay large dealers' margins as they change money. Much paperwork and costs are involved in commercial transactions.

These factors will inevitably increase the attractiveness of the

Table 3.1

Country	Exchanged	Received	Equivalent
Ireland	£100	105 punts	£100
Portugal	105 punts	2800 escudos	£98.32
Spain	2800 escudos	17.700 pesetas	£91.84
France	17.700 pesetas	800 francs	£85.45
Italy	800 francs	166.500 Lire	£84.05
Greece	166.500 lire	16.650 drachma	£83.96
Belgium	166.500 drachma	3.950 francs	£66.44
Netherlands	3.950 francs	205 guilders	£63.47
W.Germany	205 guilders	175 deutschmarks	£61.19
Denmark	175 deutschmarks	640 kroner	£59.26
Britain	640 kroner	£55.50	£55.50

Ecu as a parallel currency, both in the public and private sectors. However, if the Ecu is to be widely used it will be necessary to merge the official and private Ecu and develop it into an actual currency, with notes and coins issued for everyday use. Its basis would also have to be changed from its current dependence on the values of individual member currencies and the US $ and gold reserves which underpin it.

MONETARY UNION

Economic and Monetary Union is to be established in three stages. The first is the adoption of economic convergence programmes for price stability and sound public finance described above. The second, starting in 1994, aims at independence of national central banks and the establishment of a European Monetary Institute (EMI) to strengthen cooperation between national central banks and to coordinate their monetary policies. The Institute is to develop the use of the Ecu and a clearing system for it. Its policy is to encourage convergence of monetary policies, to bring inflation and interest rates close to each other and help keep the exchange rates of currencies within the narrow EMS bands.

By the end of 1996 the Commission and the EMI will report on progress towards economic convergence. If a majority of member states meet four convergence criteria, stage three of EMU will commence. These criteria include price stability, i.e. a rate of inflation no more than 1.5 per cent above the average of the three best performing member states; an interest rate not more than 2 per cent above the three best performing members; stable exchange rates within the ERM for at least two years; and a government debt not exceeding 60 per cent of GDP. If a majority of members meet these criteria then the European Council, by qualified majority, can decide to launch stage three. If not enough members meet them by 1997, then stage 3 will automatically come into force on 1 January 1999 for those countries that meet the criteria.

Stage three involves the setting up of a European System of Central Banks consisting of a European Central Bank (ECB) and the national central banks. Their tasks include defining and implementing a Community monetary policy, the conduct of foreign exchange operations, the holding and management of foreign reserves of member states and ensuring the smooth operation of the payments system.

With the start of stage three the participating states will irrevocably fix the exchange rates of their currencies and convert them into Ecus. The Ecu will then become a currency in its own right. The ECB will have the exclusive right to authorise the issue of Ecu banknotes and coins. Both the ECB and the national central banks will be independent and will not take instruction from either Community institutions or national governments. The governing council of the ECB will include the governors of the national central banks, a president, vice-president and four other members. The last six will be appointed by the Heads of Governments after consultation with the European Parliament. The President of the Council of Ministers and a member of the Commission will be able to participate in the deliberations of the ECB, but without a vote. The President of the ECB will also be invited to participate in relevant Council meetings. The ECB will submit annual reports on policy and activities to the European Parliament, the Council, the Commission and the European Council of Heads of Governments. The Parliament will have the right to question ECB members at appropriate parliamentary committee meetings.

TAXATION

Among the barriers creating a free and competitive market within an economic and monetary union are widely diverging national taxes. While customs duties have long been abolished, fiscal barriers continue to hamper free trade. There are divergent national VAT and excise duties. The differing levels of taxation cause divergences in production costs and selling prices. To correct these, member states have to maintain frontier formalities and controls, at which taxes are remitted on exports and imposed on imports. Apart from heavy costs caused by delays and formalities, these differences invite tax evasion and fraud, which are difficult and costly to police.

A uniform level of taxation throughout the Community might seem desirable, but American experience, for instance, shows that this is not necessary. Sales taxes vary between different states within the USA, but in practice they do not diverge by more than 5 per cent, a margin that does not appear to distort trade or prevent its free flow across state boundaries. A similar margin was suggested by the European Commission, which wanted VAT and excise duties between member states to be brought to within 6 per cent of each other. The Commission had in mind two rate bands for VAT. The standard rate of between 14 per cent and 20 per cent and a reduced one for basic necessities of between 4 per cent and 9 per cent. Member states would be free to fix the actual levels within these bands. The current standard rate of 17.5 per cent, applied in Britain, would pose no problems. Similarly, the Commission wants rates of excise duties to be approximated.

There had, however, been a lot of resistance from member states to these proposals. The objections stemmed from both political and revenue considerations. Britain and Ireland operate a zero rate on some items, including food, children's clothing and books. It had been suggested that approximation of taxes would be forced on member countries by the market itself. Leaving it to market forces, however, would invite fiscal competition between states and this would harm both trade and public revenue. Progressive approximation might be the transitional answer. Temporary exemptions might be permitted for products less sensitive to transnational competition provided that they do not involve continuing frontier controls. In the end the Council agreed in June 1991 on a minimum 15 per cent rate of VAT but also allow lower rates for special items.

The approximation of excise duties is particularly important in the case of transport. At present, much distortion of competition is caused by widely differing diesel, road and vehicle taxes, though here political objections to their harmonisation are less likely. In the case of tobacco and alcohol, objections to harmonising levels are usually based on grounds of health, where they have to be lowered, and on social habits, where they would have to be raised. Progressive approximation within agreed limits over a number of years appears to be the solution.

COMPETITION POLICY

The reason for a vigorous competition policy is that it stimulates economic activity, forcing enterprises continually to improve their efficiency. Furthermore, it guarantees free competition by preventing cartels and restrictive agreements. The Treaty of Rome outlaws deals between companies to fix prices, share out markets, place limits on investment, development and production, or adopt other restrictive practices. It bans abuses of dominant positions by firms or groups of enterprises and forbids government subsidies that distort or threaten to distort competition. The policy is administered by the European Commission, which has full powers to make sure it is observed.

A few examples will illustrate the way the Commission enforces its competition policy. Market sharing agreements have generally been banned. The first fines imposed by the Commission were in 1969 on companies operating a cartel in quinine. Sugar producers operating a cartel were fined in 1973; and more recently, in 1984, cartels of zinc and flat glass manufacturers were fined a total of Ecu 4 million (£3.2m).

Price-fixing agreements, such as the dyestuffs cartel which in 1969 controlled 80 per cent of the European market, were outlawed. Firms with head offices outside the Community were fined because they were operating within the Community in a way that was damaging to its interests.

There is a ban on agreements to buy only from specified manufacturers or importers, and to sell only to certain buyers, because they carve up the market and give unfair advantages which distort free trade. The products involved range from gramophone records to heating equipment.

Agreements, including those operated in the motor trade which seek to restrict parallel imports, are also outlawed. The Ford motor company was heavily fined for applying such agreements, as was the Moet-Hennessy champagne group, whose

British subsidiary banned UK traders from re-exporting its products. Discrimination against retailers, especially for their pricing policies, has also been severely punished.

Even in the case of agreements on industrial and commercial property rights, the exclusive use of patents, trademarks or works of art is not always exempted from competition rules. In 1982, for instance, the Court of Justice ruled against the total territorial protection granted by a patent licensing contract covering maize seed.

The policy is not, however, purely negative, but also encourages positive developments. The Commission has authorised agreements which help to improve the production and distribution of goods, or promote technical or economic progress. Being interested in cooperation between small and medium-sized enterprises, the Commission allows some types of agreement which escape the general ban. These include: exclusive representation contracts given to trade representatives; small-scale agreements involving a turnover of less than Ecu 50 million (£40m) with a market share of not more than 5 per cent; sub-contracting agreements; and exchanges of information, joint studies and joint use of plants between companies.

A major problem of competition policy is that national governments tend to shield national or local firms from competition through state aid, public ownership, preferential public procurement, special loans, export subsidies and loss write-offs. One example of the last was the British Government's attempt to write off all the accumulated losses of the Rover car company before selling it to the private sector. Many of these practices are being outlawed, but continuous policing by a vigilant Commission is necessary to prevent them happening in spite of their illegality. Disputes can be resolved by the European Court of Justice.

As we have moved to a fully integrated market, all major mergers between companies which could damage competition and consumer interests in the Community are being policed by the Commission, instead of being left to national governments. In the past the Commission has occasionally intervened, as it did in the take-over of British Caledonian by British Airways. Once the market is integrated there is, however, no further case for national governments to operate their own rules and all mergers that have a European dimension have become a Community responsibility.

European laws dealing with public companies have been enacted over many years. With the full integration of the market, different national legal systems need to be reconciled to allow the formation of genuinely European companies that can operate without hindrance throughout the Community. Many existing directives, laying down common practices, deal with disclosure, capital formation, how assets and liabilities are handled in mergers, takeovers and company closures, and company accounts and their auditing.

The question of workers' rights also affects competition. The reasons for harmonising workers' rights are twofold. First, working conditions that differ substantially from country to country can distort trade and investment. The second is the need to promote good industrial relations: these should include the right to be informed and consulted over proposed closures, moves, changes in organisation and working methods, and the introduction of new technologies. Statutory participation of workers in supervising management in both Germany and the Netherlands has created excellent industrial relations that are the envy of the rest of Europe and provide an example to be followed. In any case, for companies increasingly operating in several member states, the currently divergent rules for worker participation need to be harmonised.

The issue is largely resolved in an Agreement on Social Policy of the Maastricht Treaty, from which the United Kingdom has excluded itself. The details are covered in Chapter 4, but in essence they lay down procedures for working conditions, health and safety protection and the consultation of employees.

INDUSTRIAL POLICY

To promote free competition within an economic union requires much more than merely the removal of customs barriers. The Single European Act removed technical barriers by adopting harmonized standards for goods, for public health, safety and environmental reasons. It also established a single market in services, transport and communications, and freed capital movements.

A common policy for industry is now explicitly included in the Maastricht Treaty. To ensure its competitiveness it aims to speed up adjustments of industry to structural changes. It will encourage the development of new enterprises, particularly small- and medium-sized undertakings. It will promote trans-European networks in transport, telecommunications and energy installations. Finally, it will foster and encourage new technologies by backing cooperation in research and development.

Special concern with ensuring Europe's world competitiveness has led the Community to make particular and significant contributions to technological developments and their commercial exploitation under various Community-sponsored programmes, encouraging cooperation between universities, research institutes and commercial undertakings. The problem has been highlighted by Europe's failure to match the successes of American, Japanese, Korean and other south-east Asian competition. This has not been due to a lack of scientists of suitable calibre or shortage of resources available for research and development. In the 1970s and early 1980s Europe's expenditure on research and development matched that of the United States and was double that of Japanese expenditure. The real problem was the lack of cooperation between Community members, with each country tending to pursue independent policies that frequently duplicated research and made products that were incompatible with those of their neighbours. Not only had American, Japanese and south-east Asian technologically advanced products become dominant in international markets, but even within the Community they beat home producers at their own game. In the early 1980s, for instance, eight out of ten personal computers sold in Europe came from America and nine out of ten video-recorders were Japanese.

To try and correct this imbalance, the Community adopted a number of framework programmes for Community research and development activities. Three of these have been running consecutively from 1984 to 1994. They are addressed to speeding up the pace of technological progress and promoting competitiveness in European industry. This covers a multitude of activities in fields such as information and communications, industrial and material technologies, and the management of natural resources (such as the environment and energy) and of human resources (including the training of researchers).

But it is the removal of protectionism in public procurement and the adoption of common standards, envisaged by the Single European Act, that will be the key to the creation of a unified market for technology in Europe. Only then will it match the advantages of large home markets that both America and Japan have enjoyed for so long. A further major stimulus to technological R&D in Europe could also come from the development of a European Security Policy based on common arms procurement. Another stimulus could be learning from the Japanese example of direct government involvement in encouraging R&D cooperation between private firms in civilian markets.

THE TECHNOLOGICAL FUTURE

What of the future? Within twenty years technology will eliminate geography as a significant factor in our lives. The linking of computers and telecommunications has brought about audio-visual instant communication across the world into practically every home. Electronic mail and messages will largely replace traditional posts. Machine translation and simultaneous interpretation at the receiving end will make world-wide television accessible in all countries in their own languages. Travel will be faster, with space as an added dimension to intercontinental travel. The workplace will normally be at home with the majority engaged in service industries while robotics will largely control production. Most markets will no longer have locations but be based on network communications. Finally, information on practically every topic will be instantly accessible in the home through teletext links with databanks.

These and other developments, thanks to advanced technology, will tend, during the twenty-first century, to turn our planet into a global village, but the road to that goal may well be bumpy. Ideally we would need unrestricted transfer of technology and a world market where protection had all but disappeared. While, laudably, we are going in this direction within Europe by removing national barriers and protectionism within the Community, the same is not as true of Europe's principal competitors, the USA and Japan.

The Americans jealously guard their technology. Their 'buy American' policy discriminates against exporters to the USA. Their massive procurement programmes, confined almost exclusively to American industry by the US defence department and space programmes, have been a major source of American technological superiority, not just in defence or space-related equipment but, as a spin-off, in most industries using technologies first developed as result of defence and space contracts. The American home market of some 240 million provides a massive base for the growth of large companies that, through takeovers and mergers, have become multinational giants operating on a worldwide scale, not least in Europe itself.

The Japanese technological success does not stem from military R&D. Much of this success came from the encouragement given to private industry by the Japanese Ministry of International Trade and Industry (MITI) to exploit civilian markets. By coordinating their activities, with relatively limited financial aid, MITI persuaded Japanese companies to make a large commitment to new product development and to the capture of markets overseas. With a much larger proportion of GNP devoted to R&D than in the western economies, the resulting technological achievements have been most impressive. Operating from a large domestic base of some 119 million consumers, Japanese industry has been highly successful in penetrating markets throughout the world and particularly those of its principal competitors. At the same time, the Japanese have not been averse to protecting their domestic market from foreign incursions by various administrative measures as well as by fostering chauvinist attitudes to imports that are in direct competition with home-produced goods.

Europe's interests are not to cut itself off from the rest of the world but, equally, the Community should be just as ready as the USA or Japan to act on occasion in its self-interest. While technological collaboration with American, Japanese and other foreign or multinational firms should not be excluded, the Community should be ready to discriminate against non-European multinationals within its collaborative programmes, just as the Americans and Japanese discriminate against foreign firms. Ultimately, all such discrimination ought to disappear, but that will only be achieved on a basis of reciprocity.

Europe's capacity to match the competition will, however, depend on the successful unification of the internal market, including public procurement and the achievement of unified regulations and standards in the high-technology fields. As in the USA, these measures must, however, be combined with vigilant and tough anti-trust action. The Community must act forcefully to prevent cartels and the exploitation of dominant market positions, which cushion firms from effective competition, weaken their will to innovate and stifle the more dynamic smaller firms with new ideas. Indeed, Europe should encourage new entrants by positive discrimination in awarding public contracts to the smaller firms and ensuring that adequate new venture capital is available to them.

Finally, more public financial resources ought to be made available. A major fillip to Europe's technological effort could come from common arms procurement and a Community defence budget. The American experience of technological innovation, spearheaded and stimulated by space and defence procurement, provides a telling example of how to keep up the momentum. Once Europe starts matching her main technological rivals, its clout will help the more desirable aim of lowering barriers between them so that, together, they can spread the benefits of the new technological revolution throughout the world.

EXTERNAL RELATIONS

Completing the internal market requires the further development of its common external policy. Separate national policies for dealing with imports from outside the Community could only operate by keeping controls at frontiers to prevent trade distortions and deflections, something which is, of course, incompatible with an internal market in which frontiers have been abolished. Differing quotas, like those applied to Japanese cars, for instance, can no longer be permitted.

There is, however, an even more important case for a common external policy that is open to the rest of the world. If the Community's aim is to promote competitiveness, response to demand and innovation, then a 'Fortress Europe' approach to trade with the rest of the world would be not only illogical but liable to weaken European economic performance in comparison with its principal world competitors.

Voluntary export restraints negotiated with foreign suppliers by individual member states in the 1970s have fostered inefficiency without really being effective and have been very costly for consumers. Greater competitiveness in the Community's home market is the best way of responding to competitive pressures from the rest of the world. As the world's largest trader, the

Community's overriding interest is to fight protectionism throughout the world. By using its economic weight the Community can
enforce reciprocal access and thus stimulate international trade so
that everyone benefits.

Chapter 4

Cohesion

Removing national frontiers and creating a single barrier-free market could have damaging economic and social consequences for the weaker regions and sectors of society. This was explicitly recognised in the Single European Act. In it, a whole section was devoted to promoting and strengthening economic and social cohesion in order to ensure the Community's overall harmonious development. In particular it aims to reduce disparities between the various regions of the Community and the backwardness of the least-favoured ones. Another section, devoted to social policy, requires member states to pay particular attention to encouraging improvements, especially in the working environment. The same commitment is made to improving health and the physical environment.

The Maastricht Treaty has taken this further. It explicitly requires member states to conduct their economic policies and coordinate them with each other to achieve economic and social cohesion. The Commission is required to submit a report every three years on progress made towards cohesion and to recommend any new measures needed to advance it.

The importance of the social and regional aspects of European integration was recognised from the very beginning. The Treaty of Rome, setting up the European Economic Community in 1957, committed the signatories to the improvement of the living and working conditions of their peoples and to reducing differences between the regions of the Community. Indeed, the concept of economic and social cohesion is accepted as fundamental to all progress towards European unity. To ensure that cohesion within European society is never lost sight of, one of the statutory institutions set up by the community has been the Economic and

Social Committee, which must be consulted by the Commission and Council on most matters. Its composition is based on three groups: the first covers employers, the second workers and trade unions, the third includes other interest groups such as consumers, farmers, the self-employed, academics, etc. The Committee's work is undertaken by its specialist sections, whose recommendations are submitted for approval by the whole Committee in plenary session. The opinions arrived at must be taken into account by the Commission and Council before Community legislation is enacted. The specialist sections cover such diverse subjects as agriculture, transport, energy, economic and financial questions, industry, commerce, the crafts and services, social questions, regional development, protection of the environment, public health, consumer affairs and external relations.

If integration is to be acceptable to the poorer countries and to the public generally, there has to be a trade-off between the benefits to industry and commerce of a common market and the likely disadvantages to the weaker regions or sectors of society in a free-for-all environment. The maintenance of a balance of advantage has thus been an essential condition of all progress towards European unity.

Britain under its consecutive Conservative governments has strongly resisted extension of cohesion policies to cover workers' rights. Unlike all its partners, Britain does not appear to recognise that working conditions are an integral part of the social dimension of integration and that inequality in the treatment of workers can affect competition by denying a level playing field for commerce and industry. In particular, Britain has contested Community involvement in legislation regulating consultation between employers and workers, and has frequently objected to trade union involvement in the consultative process. Mrs Thatcher refused to accept the 1989 Social Charter and Mr Major staked his reputation on excluding Britain from the Social Chapter of the Maastricht Treaty.

AGRICULTURE

The first example of a trade-off in benefits was implicit in the agreement to develop a common agricultural policy. The French, fearing the more powerful and efficient German industry, insisted on a balancing benefit to the agricultural sector, so important to the French economy. But there was a wider consideration which persuaded the EEC's six member states to give priority to agriculture. In the 1950s nearly one-third of the Community's population was working and dependent on the land. Their living standards were no more than two-thirds of average incomes. Yet farm production was far from satisfying the full demand for foodstuffs, which had to be supplemented by substantial imports from abroad.

To deal with these problems the common agricultural policy was devised to increase agricultural productivity, ensure a fair standard of living for those working on the land, stabilise markets, guarantee regular supplies, and ensure reasonable and stable prices to consumers. The CAP has been largely successful in achieving its objectives, though with some adverse consequences not originally foreseen.

Generous price support to farmers and technical innovation have resulted in massive increases in productivity and supplies. Attracted by higher earnings in industry and with financial help from the Community, more than two thirds of the farming population has abandoned agriculture, while the average living standards of those remaining have risen sharply. The Community has become virtually self-sufficient in all but tropical foodstuffs and some animal feeds. The policy has assured price stability, though at a level generally higher than on the world market. From the consumers' point of view supplies have been secure and prices stable, untouched by periodic surges in the world price for sugar and cereals. Food prices in the Community have risen more slowly than the general price index and, with generally higher living standards, food now accounts for a much smaller proportion of people's domestic budgets than it did when the CAP was started. Food then took about 30 per cent of average budgets, whereas now the figure is less than 20 per cent.

The success of the CAP has, however, had its own costs. The system depends on guaranteed prices for most products, set each year by farm ministers. They are under continuous pressure from their own farmers to set prices at the highest possible level, which in turn stimulates production in excess of current demand. Under the CAP's guarantee system the surpluses have to be taken into stock, and from time to time, massive so-called 'butter mountains' and 'wine lakes' have been built up. Storage and disposal of the excesses has added to the budget substantially. So have the payments of export subsidies to enable European produce to be sold outside the Community at ruling world prices.

There have been justified protests from competing exporters from the USA, Argentina, Australia, New Zealand and others about the Community dumping agricultural produce on world markets. Furthermore, subsidised sales and food gifts have tended to inhibit Third World countries from developing their own agriculture.

The cost of export subsidies has at times taken up to 40 per cent of the Community's guarantee fund, whereas the total CAP budget has on average absorbed about two-thirds of the whole Community budget. Pressure to reform the CAP has consequently been growing strongly ever since 1969; and there has been some progress, although radical change has been held up by very effective national farming lobbies and the former practice of seeking unanimous agreement among ministers.

The difficulties over reforming the CAP have, incidentally, thrown into sharp relief the weaknesses of the Community's decision-making. Ministers of agriculture have defended national interests at the Community's expense, as they were not responsible for the budgetary costs. Insistence on unanimity over decisions usually resulted in compromises with little regard to cost. Proposals for reforms, regularly submitted by the Commission, have been either ignored or heavily watered down. Agriculture, the first major common policy, highlighted the fact that you cannot effectively operate policies at European level if narrower national interests take precedence over the common good.

Facing an overall budget crisis, the February 1988 European Council was finally forced to take the problem in hand. Ceilings were imposed on practically all farm products and, as soon as farmers exceeded them, automatic price cuts came into force. Total spending on the CAP was frozen, and now, if the budget is insufficient to make ends meet, the Commission is empowered to impose even more drastic price cuts.

In the light of these decisions it now looks much more likely that, over a period, agricultural supply will be more closely matched with actual demand, not just within the Community but also in world markets. At the same time there are bound to be losers among the farming community and it is here that the CAP budget's guidance section can be of major help. This, among other aids, finances programmes to help less favoured regions and mountainous and hilly areas, where it is desirable to keep farmers on the land and avoid depopulation. Other help is also made available from the European Regional Development Fund and the European Investment Bank.

The latest pressure for the reform of the CAP has come from outside the Community during the lengthy negotiations of the so-called Uruguay Round of the General Agreement on Tariffs and Trade (GATT). A sticking point, delaying agreement for a number of years, has been the insistence of other countries on a substantial reduction of agricultural subsidies by the Community. To make agreement possible, the Council finally agreed on fairly big reductions, laying the foundation for some tough bargaining between the USA and the Community. The log jam was finally broken by an agreement to limit subsidised European production of oil seeds, which were in direct competition with American producers. This paved the way for further negotiations aimed at concluding the Uruguay Round.

In the long run, agricultural support will have to be drastically reformed throughout the world. Since the 1920s farm protection has raised barriers to trade in some commodities tenfold while those for manufactured goods have fallen by three-quarters. Subsidies double incomes of farmers in the Community and the USA, and treble them in Japan. Close to US$ 100 billion is spent annually on agricultural support in OECD countries. With this support agricultural productivity has soared, while the number of those employed on the land has fallen dramatically. Yet, in spite of the overproduction of many foodstuffs, the consumers continue to pay prices well above world levels. The original objective of subsidies was to safeguard supplies in what was then a hungry world. Today, high productivity in the developed countries has removed the threat of shortages and the economic reason for subsidies has largely gone.

Some producer countries have followed the logic and now cut out subsidies altogether, as in New Zealand. After some painful adjustments its farming industry continues to thrive, remains profitable and enjoys high exports to many new markets. Without subsidies, farming is unlikely to be destroyed but would have to adapt to a competitive position, to which every other industry is exposed. The principal beneficiaries would be the consumers. What prevents any meaningful change is the remarkable political skill with which the farming lobbies are able to defend the present system of high subsidies. It needs political will, generated by more effective consumer lobbies, to confront the farmers and bring about the needed reforms. These will not come overnight, but as the numbers engaged in agriculture decline so pressure for reform will grow.

REGIONAL POLICY

The development of a regional policy followed the first enlargement of the Community from six to nine members, when Britain, Ireland and Denmark joined. The Commission found that there was considerable disparity between the poorest and most prosperous regions in each member country and within the Community as a whole. The disparity between the most prosperous and the least developed regions in the present Community of twelve in 1990, measured in terms of employment and production, was about four to one. The less privileged regions in the Community account for a quarter of its population and fall into two main groups.

First, there are the underdeveloped rural areas, largely dependent on agriculture. Incomes are low, unemployment high and most suffer from poorly developed infrastructures. They include most of Greece, Ireland and Portugal, southern Italy and Spain, Corsica and the French overseas departments. The second group covers areas where former prosperity was founded on industries that are now in decline. These are characterised by high unemployment, decaying housing and social deprivation. They are concentrated in Belgium, Britain, France and now in the eastern part of the unified Germany.

The Community's policy has three main objectives. First, to coordinate the regional policies of the member states. Second, to ensure that regional problems are fully taken into account in other Community policies. Third, to provide broad financial aid towards the development of the Community's poorer regions.

The coordination of national policies involves making certain that member states do not engage in the self-defeating practice of outbidding each other by increasing the level of national aid. Upper limits on state aids are fixed and common rules are laid down for a more coherent pattern of regional development and to avoid the waste of scarce resources.

Regional, economic and social factors are interdependent, and this calls for constant examination of the regional consequences of all Community policies. This applies in particular to the CAP, which was found to favour the more prosperous agricultural areas, and to other sector policies dealing with fisheries, shipbuilding, steel and textiles. The Social Policy and Fund have also been directed towards the needy regions.

The main element of the Community's regional policy is financial support. This comes principally from the European Regional Development Fund and from the European Investment Bank, but also from other structural aid facilities, which direct large sums towards the problems of the poorer and priority regions. The latter includes help from the Guidance section of the European Agricultural Fund for the modernisation of food production and marketing, which since its inception has given aid in excess of Ecu 12 billion (£9.6 bn). Grants and loans from the European Social Fund and the European Coal and Steel Community, totalling some Ecu 30 billion (£24 bn), have been devoted to the training and retraining of workers for the modernised coal and steel industries, and to attracting new job-creating investments. A New Community Instrument, established in 1979, provided loans for modernising infrastructure, developing energy resources and helping small and medium-sized businesses. The NCI has provided nearly Ecu 6 billion (£4.8 bn) in loans over and above the help given by the European Investment Bank.

The European Investment Bank was established under the EEC Treaty specifically to finance capital investment aimed at promoting the balanced development of the Community. Up to 1992 it had lent more than Ecu 100 billion (£80 bn), of which more than two-thirds was for developing less prosperous regions.

But the most important redistributive function is exercised through the European Regional Development Fund. From its creation in 1975 and up to 1986 it had distributed nearly Ecu 18 billion (£14.4 bn) for the promotion of economic activity and improvement of infrastructure in regions qualifying for Community aid. In the first ten years, 91 per cent of ERDF spending went to five countries: Britain, France, Greece, Ireland and Italy. After 1985 rules were changed to allocate the funds between all Community countries on a percentage basis, directed towards the least favoured regions, with the bulk going to the poorest countries – which now include Portugal, Spain and eastern

Germany. Expenditure from the ERDF accounts for 50 to 55 per cent of total costs, the rest being contributed by member states.

There are two types of programmes aided by the ERDF. There are the Community programmes designed to help solve serious social and economic difficulties in one or more regions. They group projects spread over several years, aimed specifically at Community objectives and policies. Many cover help on a cross-border basis, affecting several states. The others are national programmes of interest to the Community and fulfilling its objectives. The proposals are submitted by the member states, with the bulk of the money being allocated to individual projects put forward on behalf of local authorities, public organisations or private commercial firms.

Any major changes in policies, size or structure of the Community have their regional and social implications. In 1986, when the entry of Spain and Portugal into the Community became imminent, it was recognised that regions of member states with similar and competing economies might be disadvantaged by the removal of the preferences which, within their own countries, they had previously enjoyed. To deal with the problems, the Community introduced Integrated Mediterranean Programmes designed to help regions largely dependent on Mediterranean agricultural produce such as olive oil, wine, fruit, vegetables, etc. The IMPs apply to the whole of Greece and southern parts of France and Italy. The Community is devoting Ecu 6.6 billion (£5.3 bn) over seven years to the IMPs. Together with contributions from national and regional sources IMPs will help these countries to restructure their farming, diversify their economy and create new industrial and service jobs, especially for the young.

For the same reason – and to meet the new challenges of the barrier-free internal market and correct the economic imbalances between the richer and poorer countries that may result from the single market – the February 1988 European Council meeting agreed to double, over a five-year period, the structural funds aimed at the poorest areas of the Community. This was the trade-off necessary to ensure that the four poorest member states, Greece, Ireland, Portugal and Spain, joined in constructing the single internal market.

This doubling of the structural funds is quite apart from the new cohesion fund decided upon in Maastricht, which is to be spent on environmental projects and investment in trans-European transport networks in countries with less than 90 per cent of the average Community GDP. In any case, under the Maastricht Treaty the structural funds are to be reformed to make them more flexible, and a special protocol to the Treaty spells out other measures that could be used to promote economic and social cohesion.

The decision to create a Committee of the Regions as a new Community institution is of particular significance for the regional policy. For the first time there will be a statutory body, representing subnational government, able to participate directly in the formulation of Community policies affecting the regions and to provide a European forum where representatives or regional and local government can voice their common concerns.

SOCIAL POLICY

The Social Policy is designed to facilitate the free movement of labour, a basic principle of the Community, and to promote equal opportunities; to improve working conditions and worker participation; to promote training and education and, above all, to increase employment. Its principal instrument is the European Social Fund whose role during the economic boom period of the 1950s and 1960s was largely limited to the retraining of workers displaced through structural changes.

With the sixfold increase in unemployment between 1970 and 1986, rising to some 16 million or 12 per cent of the working population, the role of the Policy and Fund became much more significant. Extra resources were devoted to it, so that by 1986 some 7 per cent of the Community budget was allocated to the ESF, equivalent to a fivefold increase over the previous ten years.

The ESF has two main priorities. First, there are the young people under 25 for whose training and employment the Fund now spends 75 per cent of its resources. Second there are the most disadvantaged regions. Close to half of the expenditure is concentrated in seven absolute priority areas located in Greece, Ireland, Italy, Portugal, Spain and the French overseas departments.

The fight against unemployment is also directed towards easing economic difficulties that result from structural changes due to declining industries, technological modernisation or fundamental changes in demand. Help is given for retraining workers, for vocational training for the long-term unemployed and towards job-creation initiatives.

Another major concern of the Social Policy is the assurance of equal opportunities for women. Women are disadvantaged compared with men both in employment, where equality of working conditions is still a long way from being achieved, and in female unemployment, which is higher than that of the male population. The Treaty of Rome expressly laid down equal pay for equal work. Since then, new legislation has added the right to equal treatment in access to employment, training, promotion and working conditions. Furthermore, all discrimination in social security legislation is now forbidden. Positive measures are encouraged to change attitudes and attract women to occupations where they are under-represented and to higher levels of responsibility.

Improving working conditions is another major task of the Community. This involves health, safety and the working environment generally. Safeguarding rights of workers covers minimum requirements in the case of mass redundancies, the payment of salaries and other claims in transfers to other locations or occupations and a better organisation of working time. The last task includes such objectives as limiting overtime, encouraging flexible voluntary retirement and dealing with part-time and temporary work.

The free movement of labour, guaranteed under the Treaty, now applies to all occupations, except for those in the public sector concerned with security, and law and order functions. To improve conditions for migrants, national social security systems have been coordinated. Rights of association of migrants have been guaranteed. Teaching the mother tongue and the culture of young people's country of origin are now an obligation, and Community help is being considered to improve housing conditions for migrants.

The Community also concerns itself with helping the handicapped, who account for some 10 per cent of the population. It helps to promote the training and employment of handicapped people, improve their participation in social life and aid their mobility by modifying living accommodation and access to buildings.

Despite highly developed social security systems, some 30 million people are estimated to be living in dire poverty in the Community. Among them are old people, single-parent families, migrants, long-term unemployed and other marginal groups. Several Community programmes have been started to help alleviate this poverty.

The objectives of the Social Policy can, however, only be achieved through the active involvement of both sides of industry. This involves increased participation by workers in decision-making in their firms, especially in the case of multinational corporations, by obliging them to keep employees and their representatives regularly informed, and to consult them before any decisions are taken that could affect their interests. Apart from the Economic and Social Committee, the dialogue between the so-called social partners is institutionalised within the Commission's Standing Committee on Employment and in various working groups set up to study the effects of Community policies on growth and employment.

The Community Charter of Fundamental Social Rights for Workers (EC Commission 1990), adopted in the European Council in December 1989 by all Community members except the UK, spells out in detail the objectives of the social dimension in the construction of the Single Market. It recommended some fifty proposals which were being brought forward by the European Commission before the end of 1992 for adoption as an important means for the development of the economic and social cohesion of the unified market.

THE SOCIAL CHAPTER

Following Mrs Thatcher's refusal to adopt the Social Charter, it was not surprising that Mr Major resisted the further development of the Charter in the Maastricht Treaty. To overcome a potential British veto on the issue, the eleven other member states concluded a separate agreement on social policy, the Treaty's so-called Social Chapter, which will continue to be administered by the Community's institutions with Britain excluded from its deliberations and decisions. The participating states will take most decisions by a qualified majority. These will cover working conditions, health and safety of the working environment, information and consultation of workers, equality between men and women in employment and the integration of people excluded from the labour market.

Unanimous decisions will be reserved for issues of social

security and social protection of workers, particularly when their contracts of employment are terminated. It will also apply to the rights of representation and defence of the interests of trade unions and employers, including issues of co-determination. The Commission will have the task of ensuring even-handed and proper consultation with trade unions and employers at Community level.

Britain's principal objection to the Social Chapter was that its obligations would add massively to labour costs, undermine competitiveness and, as a result, lose jobs in Britain. Conversely, however, if there are such additional costs falling upon the other member states, Britain would gain unfair advantage by using cheaper labour. Indeed, recent jobs lost in France, by being transferred by their international employers to Britain, have led to French accusations of social dumping and have been referred to the European Commission as blatant breaches of fair competition. In the long run, Britain may face demands to observe a level playing field on working conditions as an essential element of the rules on fair competition. Threats of trade retaliation may then force Britain to accept the Social Chapter and legislation already enacted under it. British opposition parties support UK's participation and have made this clear during the Maastricht ratification debates.

ENVIRONMENT

Alongside concern for better working conditions, the Community is also responsible for protecting and improving the living environment. The legacy of past neglect due to lack of concern over the misuse of natural resources, bad planning and overdevelopment is still with us. Air, water and soil pollution, noise and thoughtless destruction of our fauna and flora have finally brought home the recognition that we must preserve the environment.

The Community's concern springs from the obvious fact that the natural environment recognises no man-made frontiers. Industrial waste and polluted air-streams travel across Europe. Oil slicks can affect any national coastline. Lakes and rivers extending beyond national boundaries can carry poisonous chemicals. Protection of migratory birds in one country is meaningless if they are slaughtered in another.

A common environment policy was first proclaimed at the Community's summit meeting in 1972. This was followed by three consecutive action programmes covering a wide range of measures. These include: the consideration of the impact on the environment of all other Community policies; the prevention and reduction of atmospheric, water or soil pollution; action against noise nuisances; management of waste and dangerous chemical substances and processes; promotion of clean technologies; preservation and, where possible, restoration of the natural environment and habitats needed by both fauna and flora; and cross-frontier anti-pollution cooperation within Europe and with other parts of the world. Since its start the Community has adopted more than 100 legislative acts on the environment.

To prevent water pollution quality standards have been set for sea bathing, drinking water, and fresh water and sea water suitable for fish and shellfish life. Discharge of toxic substances is strictly controlled. The Community is a signatory and participant in several international conventions aimed at reducing pollution in international waterways such as the Atlantic, the North Sea, the Mediterranean and international rivers such as the Rhine.

Anti-air-pollution measures have covered the discharge of sulphur dioxide, the use of chlorofluorcarbons in aerosol cans which can damage the earth's ozone layer, and the control of pollution from industrial premises. Member states were persuaded to accept the reduction in the lead content of petrol. Agreement has, however, been more difficult to achieve over the control of pollution from large combustion plants, particularly power stations, as well as gases from motor vehicles, which have been the main culprits of the widespread damage to forests through acid rain.

Maximum noise levels have been fixed for all types of motor vehicles, tractors, subsonic aircraft, lawn mowers and building site machinery. Further proposals are being considered for helicopters and railway vehicles.

Since the disastrous contamination by toxic dioxin in Seveso, Northern Italy, stringent measures have been taken to reduce the risks which could stem from the manufacture and disposal of chemical substances. The packaging and labelling of dangerous substances is strictly laid down. Directives control the composition of detergents, pesticides and the use of asbestos.

The collection, disposal, recycling and processing of waste is similarly subject to Community rules. Special measures apply to the control and disposal of oil and radioactive waste and to oil spillage from tankers.

Finally, several measures have been adopted to conserve wildlife, ban imports of products made from skins of baby seals, and control and restrict scientific experiments on animals. Financial support is given to projects to conserve natural habitats and further measures are planned to protect endangered species.

On the increasingly accepted principle that 'the polluter pays', Community money has been concentrated on financing pilot and research projects, conferences, seminars and technical reports based on studies which would assist the protection of the environment. Community financial resources devoted to these ends have been modest. The current programme of research has some Ecu 50 million (£40m) at its disposal. Much more substantial funds have, however, been available from the European Investment Bank by way of loans. All public and private projects that help to protect the environment are eligible, regardless of their location. In 1986, for example, more than Ecu 700 million (£560m) was lent for environmental projects.

The Maastricht Treaty spells out the objectives of the Community's policy on the environment, which include preserving, protecting and improving the quality of the environment, protecting human health, ensuring the rational utilisation of natural resources and supporting international action to deal with regional or worldwide environmental problems. Member states are to finance and implement the common environment policy, but they will also be free to apply even more stringent measures in their own countries. Where disproportionate costs are involved, affecting the poorer countries, financial support from the cohesion fund will be available.

FINANCING COHESION

Financing all the policies described above, aimed at greater cohesion within the Community, has taken the lion's share of the Community budget. In 1987, for instance, out of a total Community budget of Ecu 38.7 billion (£31 bn), agricultural, regional and social policies absorbed 79 per cent. The European Investment Bank's lending in the same year exceeded Ecu 7 billion (£5.6 bn), with the bulk going to support policies for cohesion.

The sums appear large, yet they represent less than 3 per cent of total public expenditure by the twelve member states out of their national budgets, or only about 1 per cent of the Community's gross domestic product.

Until 1988 the budget revenue consisted of four separate elements. These were: customs duties on products imported from outside the Community; agricultural levies charged on imports of foodstuffs to bring their prices up to Community levels; levies on foodstuffs intended to limit overproduction within the Community; and a proportion of value added tax which was raised to 1.4 per cent of VAT in 1986.

The new financial system adopted by the European Council in February 1988 raised the ceiling for Community funding to 1.2 per cent of GDP for payments and 1.3 per cent for commitments undertaken, or a possible budget of Ecu 60 billion (£48 bn). In addition to the VAT element, contributions from member states are adjusted in accordance with their share of total GDP. Expenditure on agriculture has finally been capped and will not be allowed to increase by more than 74 per cent of average GDP growth. Any excess will result in a reduction of prices. At the same time, spending on regional and social policies doubled by 1993.

The reform of the financial system lies in the adjustments made to VAT contributions to take account of the relative levels of wealth of member states – by linking payments to each country's GNP. This is the first significant tilt away from the Alice-in-Wonderland world in which poorer member countries are net payers while richer are net receivers, in which poorer farmers pay for richer ones and in which highly developed regions are more favoured than the less favoured ones.

The reform may thus be the very first step in the development of a European Public Finance Union, which is an essential accompaniment to the proposed economic and monetary union. When the Community originally decided in 1972 to work towards an economic and monetary union by 1980, the Commission set up a high-level study group, under the chairmanship of Sir Donald MacDougall, to look at the role of public finance in such a union. The MacDougall Report, (EC Commission 1977a) looked first at existing economic unions including five federations (Australia, Canada, Germany, Switzerland and the USA) and three unitary states (France, Italy and the United Kingdom) and compared them with the Community.

These showed that public expenditure by members of the Community averaged about 45 per cent of their GNP, whereas Community expenditure was under 1 per cent. In federal countries public expenditure at federal level, as distinct from lower levels of government, ranged between 20 and 25 per cent. It found that inequality between richer and poorer member states of the Community is at least as great as regional inequalities in income levels within the above eight countries studied, before allowing for the redistributive effects of public finance. Within these countries the redistributive effect of public expenditure and taxation is to reduce regional inequalities by 40 per cent on average.

There were significant differences between measures applied in unitary and federal systems to correct the imbalances. In unitary states the redistribution takes place almost automatically, as high incomes attract high tax payments and low incomes high receipts of centrally funded services and transfer payments. In federations, intergovernmental grants and tax-sharing play a much bigger role, achieving large redistributive effects with a relatively small federal expenditure. Furthermore, public finance in economic unions plays a major role in cushioning short-term cyclical fluctuations. A large proportion of the loss of income in a region due to a fall in its external sales is automatically compensated for by lower tax revenues to the centre and higher social security benefits.

The implications of the MacDougall findings were that, if Europe is to integrate and move to an economic and monetary union, then public expenditure at European level will have to play a much more significant role in re-distributing wealth between its richer and poorer members. This was partly recognised in 1988 by the decision to double the regional and social budgets by 1993, the date set for the completion of the internal market.

Following Maastricht, Commission President Delors was entrusted with spelling out the financial implications of the new treaty commitments and, in particular, with covering its structural and cohesion funds. After some tough negotiations at the Edinburgh European Council in December 1992, the so-called Delors II package was agreed. The cohesion fund was fixed at Ecu 15 billion (£12 bn) and the structural funds were to be progressively increased from Ecu 19 billion to 30 billion in 1999 (£15–24 bn). The funding ceiling of 1.2 per cent of GDP, agreed in 1988, was lifted to reach 1.27 per cent of GDP by 1999.

The decision of the European Council in 1992 to raise the ceiling for Community funding to 1.27 per cent of its GDP goes more than halfway towards the recommendation of the MacDougall Report for Community public expenditure to rise to 2–2.5 per cent of GDP in the so called 'pre-federal integration period.' However, MacDougall recommended that, as progress to full economic and monetary union was being made, the federal budget should rise to between 5 and 7 per cent of GDP. The target, more modest than in existing federations, is arrived at by leaving social security responsibilities in national hands. This would not, however, involve an increase in total public expenditure but merely a transfer of expenditure from national to Community levels.

From its higher income, Community expenditure could be applied principally to reducing differences between regions in capital endowment and productivity. This would help the weaker regions to improve their performance and reduce their usually higher levels of unemployment. It could be done by the Community taking a larger share than at present, of regional aid and social funding dealing with employment problems. A possible candidate for the total transfer of national public expenditure to Community level could be development aid to third countries. Another measure could be a limited budget equalisation scheme, more modest but similar to those applied in existing federations such as Canada, Germany and the USA. This aims to bring the fiscal capacity of their constituent states to around the national average.

Were responsibility for defence of the Community to be transferred to it, as may well become the case under the Maastricht Treaty's commitment to common defence, then paying for it would also become a Community responsibility. In such an event the proposed federal budget could rise to 7.5–10 per cent and provide an additional dimension to the task of moderating inequalities in wealth within the union.

Where would the additional revenue come from? One possible source is the newly reformed financial system, which relates contributions more closely to the levels of wealth of member states. As new responsibilities are transferred to the Community, contributions to finance them would have to be raised. There are other possible new sources of revenue, such as a share of corporate taxation, or a share of the social security contributions paid by individuals into a Community Unemployment Fund.

Another major source could be a carbon/energy tax, already proposed by the Commission in 1992. Although the Commission's proposals were for a neutral tax with fiscal incentives for investment in energy saving or measures to reduce carbon dioxide, they could still provide a basis for a new and important revenue contribution to the Community, which would also have redistributive effects as between the richer and poorer parts of the Community.

Another possible source could be a Community surtax on top of existing direct national taxes. Increases in revenue would, however, have to be matched by much greater accountability for its expenditure. The present institutional system of the Community lacks effective budgetary discipline. At present, Council decisions, like those of the European Parliament, are influenced by the fact that neither institution is directly responsible to national electorates for raising the taxes to pay for them. Council members and European parliamentarians are much more likely to vote for higher Community expenditure if their own country would be a net beneficiary. If, as has long been the case, there is only a small minority of members who are net contributors, the majority will continue to press for large budget increases. That is why there has been a reluctance to transfer more budgetary powers to the European Parliament or abandon unanimity in the Council on these matters.

Yet if the Community budget is to rise substantially as a share of GDP, institutional changes will have to be made to subject both revenue and expenditure to effective democratic control and make them directly accountable to the taxpayers. This might best be achieved if additional revenue were to come from the Community surtax on national taxation, as suggested above. If the surtax were clearly labelled as a European tax, individuals would become directly aware how much they pay in taxes to the Community. By acquiring budgetary powers and responsibilities equal to those of the Council, the directly elected Parliament would become much more accountable to the electorate for the financial management of the Community and for the taxes levied from them.

Chapter 5

Citizenship

What is it that could make people identify with Europe? What are the characteristics which distinguish this continent from others and which could command a greater allegiance than from peoples or countries outside it? Geographically, we are a peninsula of the Asian land mass. Our populations are drawn from several families of nations, including Anglo-Saxons, Celts, Latins and Slavs. Apart from many individual dialects, Europeans speak more than thirty distinct languages. As a result of past migrations from Europe to other continents, links between Britain and the so-called white Commonwealth, for instance, have until now been closer than with the countries across the narrow English Channel. The same applies to the sense of kinship that France enjoys with French Canada, Spain with Latin America, or indeed most Europeans with their equivalent ethnic groups in America and elsewhere.

Prior to the emergence of the European Community, the growth of nationalism in the nineteenth century and the establishment of independent, sovereign nation states after the collapse of the German, Austro-Hungarian, Ottoman and Russian empires in the twentieth century have stimulated rivalries and enmities between people of different nationalities. Within their own countries nation states have often sought to suppress ethnic minorities. To strengthen their internal unity, states have tended to centralise power at the expense of regional and local loyalties. Freedom of movement, of residence and the exercise of political and civil rights have been restricted to nationals within their own countries, thereby isolating them from their neighbours. Passports and the requirement of visas for travel abroad, introduced during the twentieth century, have symbolised the separation of Europeans of different nationalities.

To enhance their separate identities, individual nation states have laid claim to the exclusive loyalty of their citizens. Thus European history, as taught in schools, is just a long litany of conflicts between fellow Europeans of different nationalities or allegiances. In these, the cause of one's own nation is almost always portrayed as just, unlike that of one's enemies. 'Our country, right or wrong' is the phrase that best summarises the patriotism with which most Europeans have been brought up during this century.

It is easy enough to identify with the nation state. It has frontiers, national anthems, flags, postage stamps, taxes, passports and a clearly recognizable national government. Most states are associated with a national language, literature and history, which induce a natural sense of belonging.

In addition, however, the people of the European countries have a great inheritance of distinct European values that have been indelibly shaped by a common cultural and historical heritage, such as Greek thought, Roman law, Christianity and, more recently, the Renaissance with its immense influence upon architecture, literature, the arts and music, the age of reason, the industrial revolution, imperialism and social democracy. No more than a handful of countries in other continents enjoy similar standards of human rights and pluralist democracy, and, where they do, their citizens either derive their ancestry from Europe or have adopted systems that follow the example of former European imperial masters. In this broad sense there is a distinct European identity. However, apart from a shared perception of common democratic values, only students of history or the arts are likely to recognise that we have a common European heritage.

The eminent Spanish author Salvador de Madariaga, who presided over the cultural commission of the first Congress of Europe in 1948, put the objective of promoting a common European identity in the following words:

'Above all, we must love Europe; our Europe, sonorous with the roaring laughter of Rabelais, luminous with the smile of Erasmus, sparkling with the wit of Voltaire; in whose mental skies shine the fiery eyes of Dante, the clear eyes of Shakespeare, the serene eyes of Goethe, the tormented eyes of Dostoievski; this Europe to whom La Gioconda for ever smiles, where Moses and David spring to perennial life from Michelangelo's marble, and Bach's genius rises spontaneous to be caught in his intellectual geometry; where Hamlet seeks in thought the mystery of his inaction, and Faust seeks in action comfort for the void of his thought, where Don Juan seeks in women met the woman never found, and Don Quixote, spear in hand, gallops to force reality to rise above itself; this Europe where Newton and Leibniz measure the infinitesimal, and the Cathedrals, as Musset once wrote, pray on their knees in the robes of stone; where rivers, silver threads, link together strings of cities, jewels wrought in the crystal of space by the chisel of time... this Europe must be born. And she will, when Spaniards will say 'our Chartres', Englishmen 'our Cracow', Italians 'our Copenhagen'; when Germans say 'our Bruges', and creep back horror-stricken at the idea of laying murderous hands on it. Then will Europe live, for then it will be that the Spirit that leads History will have uttered the creative words: 'Fiat Europe!'.

People in general need clear and tangible concepts in order to develop a sense of belonging. And that sense of identity is an indispensable factor in achieving and maintaining European unity. Jean Monnet recognised this when, at the end of his life, he said that if he had to begin again he would start with culture. With his wide experience of international cooperation he became increasingly convinced that problems blocking the path to political and economic union cannot be solved simply by compromise between national reservations. Most of the issues on monetary, taxation, trade and other matters are overshadowed by political considerations shaped by values which largely spring from distinct cultural attitudes and identities.

The Belgian Prime Minister, Leo Tindemans, similarly stressed the importance of the cultural dimension in his 1975 report on European Union, in the following words:

The proposals for bringing Europe nearer to the citizen are directly in line with the deep-seated motivations behind the construction of Europe. They give it its social and human dimension. They attempt to restore to us at Union level that element of protection and control of our society which is progressively slipping from the grasp of State authority due to the nature of the problems and the internationalisation of social life. They are essential to the success of our undertaking: the fact that our countries have a common destiny is not enough. This fact must also be seen to exist.

RIGHTS AND FREEDOMS

What then are the factors that impinge directly on people's lives, and how have they been dealt with up to now during the process of European integration? First, there are the human rights and fundamental liberties. These were enshrined in the European Convention for the Protection of Human Rights, which formed part of the Statute of the Council of Europe set up in 1949. The European Court, established to ensure compliance with the convention, has jurisdiction binding on member states and access to it by individual citizens.

The right of free movement from one member state to another is a right guaranteed to all Community citizens. It is one of the fundamental principles of the treaties setting up the Community. This forbids all discrimination on grounds of nationality, whether relating to employment, wages, social security, trade union rights, living and working conditions, housing, education or vocational training. The only restrictions allowed on the free movement of workers are for justified reasons of public order, health and safety and for strictly defined employment in local or national public administration.

The rights include: equal pay for men and women; the right to work in the country of one's choice and to receive equal pay with workers native to that country; the right to buy and sell without being hindered by frontiers; the right to benefit from fair prices based on free competition and not on dominant market positions or monopolies; and finally the right to legal redress across Community borders.

The equal treatment principle has been embodied in a whole series of regulations, which abolish the need for a work permit, which guarantee most trade union rights, the right to education and job training, to social security payments and study grants. Enrolment and study fees must, for instance, be the same for all Community students.

Protection for women against discrimination on the grounds

of their sex has been enshrined in Community law. This legislation covers job descriptions, access to employment, training, promotion, working conditions, social security, the right of legal redress and the protection of plaintiffs against retaliatory dismissal.

Legislation to protect women against discrimination has not been enough to stop it. The European Court of Justice has made many judgments requiring employers and others fulfil their legal obligations. In 1981, for instance, the Court ruled against Lloyds Bank for refusing to give female employees under twenty-five the same pensions rights as other workers, on the grounds that an employer's pension contribution forms part of earnings. Compensation can be backdated, as was established by the Court in 1976 when a Belgian air hostess, whose pay was lower than that of male stewards, won her case.

Part-time workers are similarly protected. In a British case a lady working for a company producing women's clothes, who was earning 10 per cent per hour less than her full-time fellow workers, was judged to be subject to sexual discrimination. A similar judgment was given when a chain of Frankfurt shops refused to provide supplementary pensions for their part-time women workers.

There have been many cases of professional people wishing to practice in a country other than their own. Frequently, however, national legislation or professional rules have prevented them. In 1974, for instance, the Court judged that a Dutchman who studied law in Belgium was fully entitled to practice in that country. A few years later the Court ruled that a Belgian medical practitioner was entitled to set up a practice in Holland and a Belgian doctor of law to practice in France.

The problem was resolved in 1988 when the Council, acting to implement the Single European Act, decided that from the end of 1990 all professional people with a recognised national certificate, diploma or other professional qualification will have the right to set up anywhere within the Community. Some ten million people within the Community are affected, including teachers, librarians, lawyers, bankers, accountants, members of the medical professions, engineers, builders, foresters, etc. The new principle is that any person qualified for a particular profession in one member state will be free to practice in any of the other eleven.

The only qualification to this full freedom of establishment is the right of the host state to require a test to be taken for all those professions which require a knowledge of domestic law. This could apply to lawyers, insurers, patent agents, etc. For all other professions where there could be some divergences in training in different countries, immigrating professionals may be required to undergo a limited probationary period before being given full freedom to practice in the host state.

Community law states that migrants from another member state must be treated like nationals of the host country. This applies as much to employees as to their dependents. There have been several examples of immigrant workers who gained Court judgments in their favour. There was the case of a seriously handicapped son of an Italian who was refused welfare payments in France on grounds of his nationality. The dependent mother of another Italian worker, living in Belgium, obtained income payable in their country to retired Belgians. There have been Britons and Dutch who received Belgian benefits guaranteed to their own nationals without visible means of support. Interest-free loans payable to new parents under regional legislation in the state of Baden-Wirttemberg were judged to be equally applicable to an Italian couple working in Stuttgart.

All disputes concerning the rights of individuals under Community law are subject to the final and binding rulings by the European Court of Justice. Access to it is not limited to European Community institutions and to member states. Many of the Court's judgments stem from individuals invoking Community laws in their national courts, even in cases where a member state has failed fully to adapt its legislation to that laid down by the Community. Judges may consult the European Court of Justice for its ruling. In cases where a judicial decision cannot be appealed to a higher national court, the right of access to the European Court is guaranteed.

A further improvement to protect the rights of individuals suggests itself. A European Equal Opportunities Commission might be given the task of looking into cases of discrimination between citizens of different Community countries and those of their minority groups, where appropriate, so that these could be submitted for adjudication to the European Court of Justice.

Europeans gained some of their democratic rights within the Community with the institution in 1979 of direct elections to the

European Parliament, which take place every five years. The Maastricht Treaty has taken this further by establishing a European citizenship alongside that of national citizenships (described on p. 93).

CONSUMERS

But it is as consumers that European integration has had a rapid and major impact on the daily lives of people. The abolition of customs barriers widened the choice of goods and services, and this will now increase substantially. Prices are likely to become even more competitive now non-tariff barriers have been eliminated and since the single market became fully established in 1993.

A European consumer policy was first established when the October 1972 Summit ruled that improvement in the quality of life was the first priority of economic development. To implement this, a directorate-general for the environment and consumer protection was set up within the Commission. A Consumers' Consultative Committee was given the task of providing a forum for consumer associations to consult with each other and with Community institutions, and the Community adopted several programmes for consumers. These were designed to safeguard health and safety, protect consumers' economic interests, give value for money, and guarantee the right to redress or damages.

Health and safety protection has for long been a national concern. But differing national standards and technical regulations have often impeded the free flow of goods across frontiers. This problem was first overcome by a seminal judgment of the European Court of Justice in 1979, in the 'Cassis de Dijon' case, which established the principle that a product legally made and sold in one country should be admitted to the market of every other member state. This principle was accepted as a basis for the completion of the single internal market.

Consumers are also protected through a wide range of Community directives covering food products and their purity. Regulations govern the composition, manufacture and naming of honeys, jams, marmalades, fruit juices, mineral waters, tinned milk, cocoa and coffee products. Rules are also laid down for the presentation, labelling and packaging of foodstuffs. Other goods subjected to regulations for consumer protection include cosmetics, textiles, pharmaceuticals, dangerous substances and manufactured goods such as cars and tractors.

Since 1984 member states have been obliged to inform the Commission and other member states of any serious accidents requiring urgent measures to protect the health and safety of consumers and prevent future accidents. This is particularly relevant to children's toys, which may contain lead, for instance, or other dangerous products. To this end the Commission publishes guides on accident prevention.

Protection against dishonest and improper trading practices is another area of Community concern. Directives have been issued on misleading advertising, door-to-door sales, manufacturer's responsibility for damage caused by a defective product, on consumer credit, the importation of counterfeit products and on redress available to consumers.

The Community has been improving consumer representation by financial grants to stimulate the creation and strengthening of consumer associations in member countries that lack them or where they are weak. In addition, four all-European organisations, whose role is to lobby for improvements in Community consumer policy, get financial assistance. They are the bureau for consumer associations (BEUC), the confederation of associations dealing with family matters (COFACE), the European Trades Union Confederation (ETUC) and the Community organisation for consumer cooperatives (EUROCOOP). A Consumers' Consultative Council has been established to advise the Commission on consumer protection and on the formulation of other relevant legislation.

TOURISM

Travel and tourism within Europe have become big business. Some 20 per cent of people who take holidays, go to another Community country. Most travel by road, others by rail, air or on water. Tourism represents some 5 per cent of the Community's GDP and 8 per cent of private consumption. It provides the equivalent of 5.5 million full-time jobs and, being a major growth area, it can make an important contribution to creating new jobs and developing backward regions.

Yet among the most irritating experiences of tourism across Community borders have been long delays while passports were

checked and travellers questioned by customs officers in what was
supposed to be a customs-free Community. The Single European
Act has finally ended these barriers, though some checking of
passports continues, especially on entry into the United Kingdom
from the Continent, on the grounds that non-Community citizens might otherwise slip in. This anomaly illustrates the need for
a common immigration policy that might emerge under the
Maastricht Treaty's new responsibilities for Justice and Home
Affairs.

Emergency medical care, on the same conditions as that provided to their own nationals, is now available to all Community
citizens. A European emergency health card has been devised,
which contains medical information in all languages necessary
for the safety of such travellers as diabetics or with a heart
condition. Access to legal aid is also available to those visiting
another Community country.

Duty-free allowances have been substantially increased and
insurance companies must now provide third party cover for
motorists and their families travelling to other Community countries. Finally, a Community driving licence has been introduced
and all driving licences issued by member states must now conform to the Community model.

Community financial aid plays an important role in expanding
tourism in member countries. Between 1980 and 1986 the European Investment Bank gave low-interest loans totalling Ecu 350
million (£280m) for more than 1000 tourist projects. Among the
most notable have been loans to restore and maintain important
cultural monuments such as the Doge's Palace in Venice and the
Parthenon in Athens. Grants from the European Regional Development Fund totalling Ecu 326 million (£240m) during the same
period have also aided some 660 tourist projects, including holi-
day villages, pleasure harbours, ski lifts, hotels, sport and
conference centres, bathing resorts, museums and archaeologi-
cal sites.

Finally, the Community is directly concerned with improving
working conditions for those engaged in the tourist industry.
Studies have been financed to examine employment in hotels,
restaurants and cafes, and to standardise computer vocabularies
and access to data banks for hotel reservation systems. Community directives lay down that all jobs in the tourist industry,
including interpreters, couriers and guides, can be practised by

Community citizens in any country of their choice. Help is available for vocational training abroad, particularly important for language practice.

EDUCATION

The whole issue of education plays a central role in the Community's strategy to train people for work outside their own country. But the principal role of the Community's education policy is to promote better mutual understanding and the growth of a European consciousness.

Many people believe that the biggest barrier to unity is the fact that Europeans speak so many languages. True, but so do the polyglot citizens of Russia or India. The latter in particular offers a good example to Europe. The Indian Union's two official languages are Hindi and English. The constitution also recognises fifteen main languages used for official purposes within individual states. All India Radio broadcasts in fifty-one languages and eighty-two tribal dialects. Of course there is a natural desire to ensure that the use of one's own language is not diminished and that its cultural heritage, in the form of literature, does not atrophy. That is certainly not the aim or intention of European integration.

There is, however, the problem of the high cost of translations and interpretation within Community institutions. With twelve member states there are nine official languages and under existing rules all documents have to appear in them. Interpretation into all the languages has also to be provided for most meetings. The problem will not become easier once the Community is further enlarged.

In the Council of Europe, with more than thirty member and associated countries, the accepted official languages are English and French. To adopt this practice within the Community institutions may not be easy, but it has been suggested that, in fairness to the others, people should not use their own mother tongue. This would mean that the French would have to use English and the British, French. Whatever the wishes of those anxious to preserve their own tongues, the trend in Europe and throughout the world seems to be towards the universal use of English for international communication.

Nevertheless, the Community is committed to preserving

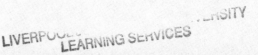

multilingualism as a feature of its cultural richness. To do this it encourages language teaching, for which guidance and financial help is given. Schools are recommended to teach not less than two other languages. Help is also given in the translation of major literary works originally written in minority languages.

Beyond the knowledge of foreign languages, a most important contribution to mutual understanding and the building of a common European consciousness lies in the teaching of European history. In virtually every country the history taught in its schools has a hoary accumulation of subjective national bias, often hostile to its neighbours, that should now be weeded out. Over a period, national history curricula ought to be redesigned to ensure that national history is taught within the context of its wider European and world framework.

Under the Maastricht Treaty the Community is to contribute to the development of quality education by encouraging cooperation between member states and by supporting and supplementing their activities. This includes developing a European dimension in education, which encourages mobility of students and teachers, cooperation between educational establishments, and youth exchanges. It is also committed to a vocational training policy which helps to adapt workers to industrial change. Finally, its role is to foster educational cooperation with third countries (that is, non-community countries) and with appropriate international organisations.

The Community operates four educational programmes to implement some of the above aims. A programme adopted in 1987 under the name ERASMUS (European Community Action Scheme for the Mobility of University Students) promotes student mobility and cooperation in higher education across national borders. Finance is given to help establish inter-university cooperation programmes, covering language courses, translations and travel and subsistence for teachers while abroad. The 1992/3 budget for ERASMUS was Ecu 100 million (£80m). The LINGUA programme, established in 1989, promotes the teaching and learning of foreign languages within the Community. Finance available for the period of 1990–94 was Ecu 200 million (£160m). A programme stimulating cooperation between universities and enterprises in training for the new technologies, under the name COMMETT, was first established in 1986. Finance for 1990–94 was Ecu 230 million (£184m). Finally, there is the TEMPUS scheme (Trans-European Mobility

Scheme for University Studies). This was adopted in 1990 to help develop higher education in Central and Eastern Europe through cooperation with European Community universities. It also encourages cooperation between universities and enterprises. Finance made available for the academic year 1993–94 amounts to Ecu 107 million (£85m).

EXCHANGES

To reduce ignorance of each other's countries, languages and cultures more is necessary than just better education in schools. By far the best way to get to know one's neighbours is to visit each other. And here organised exchanges between people can play a vital role, particularly when young people go to stay with a family in another country.

Many motorists are struck by the Council of Europe signposts at the entry to towns and villages, which announce their twinning with other European places. Although such twinnings have often seemed to be confined to bilateral junketings of the respective Mayors and the chief executives, many local authorities have developed links well beyond the official exchange of visits and information. These include parallel twinning arrangements between local schools, trades councils and voluntary bodies concerned with sport and leisure activities. Exchange visits, joint events and holidays involving people in the twinned localities, particularly if well covered in the local press, can contribute effectively to mutual understanding and the reduction of narrow-minded parochialism.

But it is exchanges between young people that are likely to make the biggest long-term impact. The best illustration has been the intensive and well-financed programme of bilateral youth exchanges between France and Germany, which started in the 1950s. Millions of French and German young people have participated in the well-designed programmes aimed at removing the traditional rivalry and hostility that characterised their countries' relations over the centuries. The results have been most impressive. The hostility and suspicion, which can still be found among those who, as adults, lived through the last war, have totally disappeared among the younger generations.

To this end the Community has promoted a programme open to all young Europeans, called YES (youth exchange scheme).

The project, which started in 1988 with a budget of Ecu 30 million (£24m) promotes exchanges for some 80,000 young people between the ages of 15 and 25. They spend at least one week in another Community country, having been first prepared by suitable instruction about the economic, social and cultural aspects of the country to be visited. It is to be hoped that the scheme will be much extended, with adequate financial resources to match the excellent results achieved with the Franco-German experience.

A COMMON IDENTITY

But building a European consciousness must extend well beyond the education of our young. It needs to permeate everyday concerns and interests of Community citizens, including sport, cultural pursuits and television. In June 1984, the European Council set up an ad hoc committee for a people's Europe. It was asked to suggest ways of strengthening the identity and improving the image of the Community. Under the chairmanship of Pietro Adonnino, the committee submitted two reports which were approved by the heads of governments (EC Commission 1985a).

Among its many proposals the committee recommended the introduction and development of a Community dimension to sport. As a consequence the Community now sponsors cycling tours and European tennis, football, swimming and other sport championships. A 'Sail for Europe' Association has organised round the world cruises and Tour de France yacht races crewed by young sailors drawn from several member countries. European driving rallies and 'walks for Europe' have also taken place.

With millions of people following sport, the promotion of European sporting events has made an important contribution to mutual understanding, despite the deplorable examples of football hooliganism that have marred some events. Indeed, the shame such behaviour has generated nationally has strengthened ties through efforts to make amends. There were, for instance, significant gestures of reconciliation made through exchange visits of goodwill between the English and Italians following the tragic loss of Italian lives after the Heysel Stadium football riot in Belgium.

The creation of a European cultural area is another desirable objective. The aim is the free circulation of cultural goods and services. This covers the free movement of works of art, with business sponsorship being encouraged to mount major European exhibitions and shows. Better living and working conditions for artists as well as more information about cultural Europe are other objectives. Promotion of cultural activities in the regions is helped with Community grants and by the designation of 'European Cities of Culture'. The sponsorship of the European Symphony and Chamber Youth Orchestras has led to the creation of ensembles of high professional competence that have delighted audiences throughout the world.

Under the Maastricht Treaty the Community is now explicitly committed to contributing to the flowering of the cultures of the member states and to promoting the common cultural heritage, with full respect for national and regional diversities. Community action is directed at preserving Europe's cultural heritage, supporting artistic and literary creativity and helping cultural exchanges.

The most important role in promoting a European consciousness is that of the media, with television obviously playing a decisive part. With the proliferation of television satellites, programmes will be beamed simultaneously into homes throughout Europe. Technological developments are taking place to establish one television market with a single European television standard. By 1995 there may be up to 200 TV channels available in Europe. If these are not to be dominated by the Americans, the Community must ensure the establishment of multinational and multilingual European television programmes and stations. With suitable technological development it should soon be possible to provide satellite television broadcasts beamed simultaneously in different languages according to the viewers' choice.

The question of the financing, production and distribution of such broadcasts is already the subject of the Community's MEDIA programme. In the field of fiction series for TV, the MEDIA programme is helping to finance the Geneva-Europe prize for scripts. A European Group of Cinema and Audio-Visual Financiers was established in 1987 to help finance European co-productions. The Community hopes to assist in the setting up of a European cooperative for the distribution of low-budget films.

The 1988 European Cinema and Television Year, jointly

organised by the European Community and the Council of Europe, set out to draw the attention of the public – and of professional and political circles – to film and television as a means of promoting Europe's originality, identity and creative potential. It included symposia on European co-productions and co-distribution, as well as on pirating of audio-visual works. Several European film prizes will be awarded in future.

SYMBOLS OF UNITY

Symbols can play an important part in encouraging people to identify with the European Community. The adoption in 1986 of the old Council of Europe flag, consisting of a circle of twelve gold stars on a blue background, has helped. So could increasing use of the European anthem – the prelude of the 'Ode to Joy' from Beethoven's Ninth Symphony. Every ninth of May is now celebrated as Europe Day, commemorating the 1950 Schuman Declaration which gave birth to the Community.

The Community now also has a common passport, even if it did take some ten years of argument to agree on its colour and format. Useful though this may be to identify European citizens beyond Community borders, do we really want a passport to cross what since the end of 1992 are supposed to be non-existent frontiers within the Community? Increasingly, people find it necessary to carry some form of identity card, even if having and carrying them is not compulsory in every country. Nowadays many already carry driving licences, credit cards and travel passes. Would it not be preferable if every European citizen were issued with a common identity card with a photograph, which they could use instead of a passport for travel within the Community?

The adoption of a single European currency, discussed in Chapter 3, will naturally have a most significant impact on people's identification with the Community; as would, though less favourably, a European tax as suggested in Chapter 4. Also highly effective would be the setting up of a genuine European government.

COMMON JUSTICE

The abolition of internal frontiers has made it essential to extend the Community's competences to new areas which had hitherto been the exclusive concern of member states. Two matters in particular need common policies and action. The first covers entry into the Community of third country nationals and their treatment. The second involves crime, especially that which knows no frontiers. To deal with these matters the Maastricht Treaty includes a special chapter covering cooperation in the fields of justice and home affairs.

Like the Treaty's provisions on a common foreign and security policy, justice and home affairs are to be managed outside the normal framework of the Community's institutions and, in particular, will paradoxically not be subject to the European Court of Justice. The basis will be intergovernmental cooperation. The European Commission is to be associated with the work and the European Parliament will be consulted. The final word, however, will remain with member governments acting by unanimous agreement in the Council of Ministers, except on procedural matters where a qualified majority of at least eight member states will apply.

The new responsibilities will cover the whole issue of asylum, immigration policies and the movement of third country nationals within the Community. With the abolition of internal frontiers it will no longer be possible to apply differing national policies towards non-Community citizens and their rights of residence or employment. The new tasks will be to work out common policies on these matters.

Similarly, combating crime is an area where, without effectively policed internal borders, cooperation across these borders them is essential. This will mean close police cooperation, particularly in combating terrorism, drug trafficking and other forms of international crime, like fraud. To achieve this a European Police Office (Europol) will be established for the exchange of information, and cooperation will also be encouraged between national customs services. As a direct consequence, judicial cooperation in both civil and criminal matters will also be developed, though this will not affect the existing responsibilities of member states with regard to the maintenance of law and order and the safeguarding of internal security.

EUROPEAN CITIZENSHIP

There is little doubt that the emergence of the European Community and its growing integration has eroded some of the shackles and restraints which nation states had been imposing on their citizens. There is also evidence that people are becoming more conscious of a common European identity and that this need not conflict with continuing national, regional or local loyalties. Regular opinion polls conducted throughout the Community show a growing understanding that European unity does not involve the sacrifice of national cultural identity. Indeed, the European Union is increasingly recognised as the best guarantee for the preservation of Europe's most precious characteristic and asset – its cultural diversity. But what has been missing until recently was an explicit recognition of this emerging common identity.

The Maastricht Treaty has started to provide this by conferring a European citizenship upon every national of a member state. The Treaty enshrines the principle of total freedom of movement and residence within the the territory of member states, and offers citizens protection by the consular authorities of any member state when they are outside the Union. Other provisions include the right to be a candidate and vote in local and European elections in the country of residence, and the right to petition the European Parliament and complain to the European Ombudsman.

Welcome though these provisions are, they remain very limited and should be extended to become more meaningful to the ordinary citizen. In particular the right to vote and be a candidate should be extended to national elections in the country of permanent residence. If European citizens are free to live under the law anywhere in the Union and are obliged to pay taxes, then surely they should be given all the democratic rights which accompany such freedoms and duties. The demand for no taxation without representation is as relevant to the European Union as it was to the American colonies who fought to create their own union.

But there are other rights, some already recognised within the existing Community treaties and legislation, which need to be explicitly enshrined in an intelligible form easily understood and identified by all European citizens. The Union needs a written constitution and one that spells out in detail all the rights conferred on its citizens. These should be comprehensive and might be embodied in a Charter of Citizens' Rights forming an essential part of the proposed constitution. Many of them are already the responsibility of member states, but if we are to have an agreed common level of legally enforceable rights a European Charter is needed to provide the basis. The following fourteen points spell out the basic aims of the proposed Charter:

1 Promotion of good relations throughout the European Union between people of different races and ethnic groups.
2 Respect for the rights and cultural identities of minorities.
3 A ban on all forms of discrimination whether on grounds of race, creed, colour, nationality, sex, age, disability, or sexual orientation.
4 Formal adhesion of the European Union to the European Convention for the Protection of Human Rights and Fundamental Freedoms and the revision of Article L of the Maastricht Treaty which excludes the Convention from the jurisdiction of the Court of Justice.
5 Adequate representation of European citizens in the political structures of the European Union, by introducing a uniform electoral system, increasing the powers and responsibilities of the European Parliament and improving the democratic accountability of the European institutions.
6 The right of citizens to participate in political decisions affecting their daily lives in the member state where they are resident.
7 Provision of educational, health and social services and access to cultural, transport and public facilities, so that all may live in an open community.
8 Access to easily intelligible information and advice concerning citizens' rights under European law, and effective access to legal remedies in the event of such rights not being respected.
9 Provision for the special needs of women to enable them to take full advantage of their rights as equal citizens.
10 The right of children to care, protection and education wherever they may live in the territories of the European Union, and to be treated as full human beings, while respecting the values of family life.
11 The right of senior ('third age') citizens to adequate subsistence to enable them to maintain a decent standard of life according to their circumstances, and to equality of treatment when in other member states.

12 Special provision for disabled people, including the right to participate in the making and implementation of decisions affecting their own lives, with the aim of enabling them to enjoy equal status and opportunity with their fellow citizens.
13 The right to examine and, if inaccurate, to correct any personal information or data concerning oneself.
14 Protection of consumer interests including health, safety and quality of food and industrial products, and the right to live in decent surroundings free from damaging pollution from industrial or agricultural processes.

The above provisions, if embodied in an appropriate form in a European Constitution, adopted during the next review of the Treaty in 1996, would spell out for all European citizens the meaning of belonging to the Union and, more than any other measure, encourage them to identify themselves with it.

Chapter 6

A federal democracy

As a result of the technological revolution ever more rapid change has become the norm. Since the Second World War, modern industrial society has become much more complex and its management has led to a massive increase of government involvement in people's daily lives. Economic management, physical planning and environmental control, transport and communications, and social, health and welfare provisions are all relatively new concerns of government. They require a vast and complex machinery to administer. And so, in modern industrial countries, public-sector expenditure accounts for close to half of their gross national product. Most of these new responsibilities and powers have gone to national governments and central administrations.

This centralisation leads to functions and resources being accumulated in relatively small geographic locations, usually within easy reach of metropolitan areas and especially around national capital cities. These dominate the rest of the country, relegating vast parts to a peripheral and subsidiary role. Such concentration is not confined to government functions but inevitably extends to commerce and industry, to culture and centres of excellence, all of which want to be close to where power and money reside.

Within the European Community such concentration of functions and resources has occurred in the triangle between London, Paris and the Ruhr. Cities like Athens, Milan and Naples have also grown in all directions, attracting people, wealth and activities away from the countryside and the smaller towns and villages. The trend has had serious consequences.

The peripheral areas remain underdeveloped, culturally

deprived and increasingly depopulated. The metropolitan conurbations, congested and expensive, have turned into
maelstroms of feverish activity. City centres have become increasingly dehumanised, where mental illness, drugs and crime have
escalated.

Many local communities have lost their sense of identity. With
decisions about their lives taken, usually far away, by faceless
bureaucracies, people have become increasingly alienated from
their governments. Democratic accountability of national governments to their citizens through elected representatives has
become tenuous. Parliaments find it ever more difficult to check
the activities of burgeoning administrations. Representative democracy, meant to give ordinary citizens a say in their lives, is
becoming discredited through growing cynicism about politicians. A sense of community has been replaced by a general
feeling of 'them and us' as the gap between government and
governed has alarmingly widened.

One consequence has been the proliferation of single issue
politics, campaigns and demonstrations. Traditional methods of
democratic control through elected representatives have been
increasingly marginalised. Representative democracy is being
undermined and questioned as people demand direct participation in the decision-making process.

In most of the modern industrialised countries existing institutions are failing to respond to the needs and demands of
ordinary citizens. Rapid change in our technological society and
the massive increase in governmental responsibilities clearly require that our institutions adapt to the new circumstances if
democracy is to survive. What is needed in particular is much
greater flexibility and the diffusion of over-centralised powers.

Some European countries have managed to avoid the worst
features of alienation and the discredit of existing democratic
processes. Switzerland, for instance, provides a remarkable contrast. People in their local communities feel they belong and have
a clear say over most decisions that affect them, be it at local,
regional or national level. Both direct and representative democracy operate alongside each other. Frequent referenda are used
as a guide to elected representatives governing villages, towns,
cantons and the whole Swiss Confederation.

Plebiscites and referenda, discredited in Nazi times, have no
such place in the Germany of today. Yet the sense of community

and a strong attachment to democratic processes is characteristic of German society. Villages and towns are well administered by elected representatives and people feel very much part of their local communities. Regional governments, established after the war and exercised at Laender level, have extensive responsibilities and powers under the control of their state parliaments. The federal government is subject to wide constitutional checks and balances. As a reaction and revulsion against the Nazi era, post-war Germany has become the most stable and probably the strongest bastion of representative democracy in Europe.

THE FEDERAL SYSTEM

What distinguishes Germany and Switzerland from other western European states is that they are both federations. Within them power is distributed between the different levels of government. The distribution is based on the principle of subsidiarity, according to which all governmental decisions are taken at the lowest level possible and closest to the citizen. Each tier of government is furthermore democratically accountable to representative parliaments or assemblies elected directly by the public. The powers of the lower tiers of government are constitutionally guaranteed against encroachment by the higher levels. While each tier enjoys autonomy in the functions and responsibilities allocated to it, many powers are shared and coordinated. Disputes are usually resolved by reference to a Federal Tribunal in Switzerland, and to the Federal Constitutional Court in Germany.

Professor Maurice Vile defined federalism as a system of government in which central, regional and local authorities are linked in a mutually interdependent political relationship; in this system a balance is maintained so that neither level of government becomes dominant to the extent that it can dictate the decisions of the others, but each can influence, bargain with, and persuade the others (Vile 1973).

With the massive increase of governmental functions and responsibilities, the advantages of their diffusion have been recognised in many European countries. Devolution of powers from the centre has taken place in Italy, largely in reaction against the overcentralised state under fascist rule. The state has been territorially decentralised to grant substantial local autonomy not only to provincial and communal councils but also to an intermediate tier of regional government. More recently, in reaction to the corruption of the traditional national political parties, a new trend towards further decentralisation has manifested itself. New parties have emerged. The Lega Lombarda, for instance, after championing the effective detachment of Northern Italy from being governed from Rome, has become a national movement committed to an Italian federation with real regional autonomy and self-government.

Belgium has a strong local government tradition, with its existence guaranteed by the constitution. There are two tiers of local government, exercising a general competence under the supervision of the national government. The linguistic divisions between Flemish and French speaking areas have recently led to the federal division of the country into three autonomous self-governing regions.

The Netherlands, although a unitary state, has a well-established system of local government, consisting of eleven provinces and 842 municipalities, each with elected councils, to which in recent years the national government has consciously transferred powers previously exercised centrally.

Decentralisation has also taken place in Denmark and France. The latest French reform has created directly elected regional councils with new powers to levy their own taxes, employ staff and administer their own projects. Since the re-establishment of democracy in Spain, the highly centralised state has been transformed into a federation of seventeen regions, each with its flag, capital, government and parliament, and in the case of Catalonia its own official language. Indeed the trend, practically throughout western Europe, has been decentralisation with a steady shift in the weight of the public sector towards sub-national levels of government.

Britain alone has moved against this trend. Pressure for regional devolution, be it to Scotland, Wales or the other regions of England, has been strongly resisted by successive Conservative governments. Democratically elected metropolitan authorities for London and other major conurbations have been abolished. Local government is being emasculated, with powers increasingly concentrated at the centre, where national ministers and their civil servants have the final say. In the absence of a written constitution, the status of local government has in the past relied on convention, with its legitimacy as a proper part of the democratic system dependent on consensus politics. Under the Thatcher administration terms such as consensus and cooperation were no longer fashionable and the principle that Westminster knows best continues to be the dominant characteristic of the John Major administration.

THE EUROPEAN DIMENSION

Against this background of a general diffusion of powers from the centre to regional and local tiers in most European countries except Britain, a new dimension to the issue of the distribution of powers has arisen with the creation of the European Community. As the story of its evolution (recounted in Chapter 2) has demonstrated, the Community's institutions are continually evolving as they acquire new responsibilities. Each stage in its evolution from the very first European Coal and Steel Community has been seen as yet another step in what Robert Schuman in 1950 described as: 'laying the foundations of a European federation', described by others as a European Union or the United States of Europe.

What is often not realised by protagonists of federal devolution within nation states is that the federation of such states into larger entities is merely the other side of the same coin. It is part of a coherent system concerned with the whole range of interdependent levels of government, each democratically accountable to its own elected representative councils, assemblies or parliaments with constitutionally guaranteed powers. Thus, the attempt to federate Europe can be seen as the response to the changing nature of society, brought about by its growing interdependence and complexity in the wake of the technological revolution, which is echoed by demands for devolution of powers within nation states towards democratically accountable and autonomous regional and local authorities.

Semantic arguments about the description to be given to the process of European integration are in themselves not very important. Its substance is. As Edward Heath, in the inaugural Lothian Memorial Lecture in November 1987 put it: 'the Community was created by the founding fathers as an institution sui generis.' He did not believe that it was very productive to spend time arguing about federalism and its many different definitions. The final form of the Community's political organisation will be *sui generis*, and he urged that one should instead concentrate on making the Community a success in all its different forms (Heath 1988).

Edward Heath's view is understandable when expressed in Britain, where federalism has for many people long been a dirty word. The aversion is surprising, because federal ideas and their practice play a distinct part in the British political tradition. Towards the end of the First World War, for instance, serious consideration was given by the British government to a scheme of Irish home rule, which would fit in with a federal plan designed to facilitate Home Rule all round in the United Kingdom. It surfaced more recently during the devolution debates in the mid-1970s and is still one of the options considered for the solution of the Irish problem.

As the Empire was being transformed into a Commonwealth, the British successfully fathered federations all over the world, including Australia, Canada, India, Nigeria and Malaysia, and somewhat less successfully in Rhodesia and the West Indies. Federal Union, founded in Britain and backed by leading politicians and academics at the outbreak of the Second World War, played a seminal role in the development of plans and ideas that led to the creation of the European Community. And the Anglo-French Union proposed by Churchill and his government in June 1940 would have created a federation.

British hostility to the federal idea was fomented by establishment figures who opposed British participation in the building of the European Community after the Second World War. Since Britain joined the Community, those who want to resist the development of its institutions have played on the belief that British cultural values would be submerged within an alien continental European tradition.

The fear that we would all become foreigners is a major public misconception of federalism in its application to European unity. In a more recent speech to the European Parliament, the Queen of the Netherlands pointed out that it is a common mistake to regard the political development of the European Community as a 'development comparable to the evolution of a nation state'. Social homogeneity and cultural standardisation are not part of the Community's purpose. On the contrary, the whole history of European integration since the 1950s clearly demonstrates that the aim of the Community is to preserve and enhance Europe's social and cultural diversity. Indeed, the very essence of federalism is a federal constitution that safeguards the autonomy and integrity of its component states. This is to prevent the cultural identities of individual countries being subsumed, as they surely would be, were they to merge into a super-state without constitutional guarantees.

Part of the confusion is generated by the uncertainty about the form a future European federation might take. Many people imagine that advocates of the United States of Europe wish to replicate the system operated within the USA. Yet there are many different federal systems in existence in other parts of the world, each with its own distinct structure, adapted to the needs and wishes of its founders. Thus the USA has a presidential system under which the executive is separate from the legislature. Canada retains the British monarch as the head of state. Its government consists of a prime minister and cabinet chosen, as in Britain, from the House of Commons. The members of the upper chamber, the senate, are appointed like members of the House of Lords by the monarch, through his representative, the Governor-General. Unlike the British system, however, the two chambers enjoy equal powers. The provinces have single-chamber legislatures from which its governments are chosen.

Australia has a similar federal system, but their senate is directly elected. Their provincial territories, each operating under separate constitutions, have two-chamber legislatures, except for Queensland.

The Indian federation resembles those of Canada and Australia, though its organisation has been adapted to take account of the wide diversity of ethnic character, language and religion of its huge and mainly rural population.

The most decentralised federation is Switzerland, where the bulk of governmental powers is exercised by its component cantons, each with its own constitution and laws, and an executive drawn from an elected legislature. Sovereignty resides in the 23 cantons and the federal government exercises only those powers which have been vested in it by the constitution of the federation, drawn up by the cantons. Changes in the constitution require approval by a majority of all federal voters in a referendum, and a majority of voters in a majority of cantons.

It is of course a fact that the former Soviet Union and Yugoslavia were also federations consisting of autonomous republics with their own constitutions. But they were both highly centralised countries with totalitarian regimes handing down decisions to their component states and exercising power over their subjects, who were without any real choice in the way they were governed. Their collapse demonstrates that federalism, based on the principle of subsidiarity – that is, decisions taken as close to the citizens as is practicable – can only survive on the basis of a genuine democratic choice exercised from below. The internecine wars in former Yugoslavia and in some former Soviet republics also underline the absence in those countries of any traditional observance of fundamental human rights and their guarantee under the law.

The diversity of federal systems stems from the historical origins and distinctive cultural backgrounds of each federation and none can be regarded as necessarily the correct model for the European Community to follow. It is in this sense that Edward Heath was right to claim that Europe's political organisation will be *sui generis*, but there is little doubt that its development will be on federal lines.

The European Community has many federal features already. Its constitution consists of the treaties that set it up and the many institutional reforms introduced during its existence. The latest among these were the Single European Act and the Maastricht Treaty. The guarantor and interpreter of the constitution is the European Court of Justice, whose judgments are binding on all member states as well as on its citizens. The Community's Council of Ministers has the power to pass laws that override national legislation and are binding on all. It has a directly elected Parliament with supervisory powers over the European Commission, the governing organ of the Community; it has the final say on the Community's budget and, increasingly, it participates in the legislative process.

The Maastricht Treaty has taken the European Community further towards a federal goal. Although mention of federalism was omitted from the text at British insistence, it was replaced by 'an ever closer union... in which decisions are taken as closely as possible to the citizen'. This objective is to be achieved by Community action taken in accordance with the principle of subsidiarity. Although for most of Britain's partners the change was merely semantic, as for them subsidiarity is synonymous with federalism, it was agreed to try and define it more comprehensively. This was done at the Edinburgh European Council meeting in December 1992, which confirmed the federal orientation of those parts of the Treaty dealing with European Community functions but not with regard to the two intergovernmental chapters, one dealing with Foreign and Security Policy and the other concerned with Justice and Home Affairs. More explicitly, subsidiarity cannot be used to challenge the primacy of Community law and its control by the Court of Justice. Even on those chapters which remain outside Community competence, intergovernmental action has to respect Community objectives. On functions of exclusive Community competence, such as competition policy, enforcement of Community law and accountability for Community expenditure, subsidiarity will not apply.

Nevertheless, the Community's institutions are still some distance from providing a European government with real democratic accountability and real, if limited, powers which would transform the Community into a federation or union, to the creation of which most member countries have repeatedly declared that they are committed. What further changes would then be required for the objective to be achieved? First, there is need for the Community's competences to be extended to those matters which, under Maastricht, remain subject to intergovernmental management. They, will probably become integrated within the Community's single institutional framework after the next review of the Treaty in 1996. But even with its present responsibilities an examination of the structure, functions and powers of each institution will illustrate its strengths and weaknesses, and indicate where reform could make it more effective.

THE COMMISSION

The Commission is the executive organ of the Community. Its members, although appointed by national governments, are under no obligations to them, and their loyalty, expressed in an oath on taking office, is pledged to the Community alone. At present the Commission consists of seventeen members, two each from the five larger states and one each from the seven smaller countries. They are appointed by their national governments for four-year terms, which are renewable. The President of the Commission is appointed for renewable two-year terms by all the member governments jointly. Each commissioner is allocated an area of responsibility, usually proposed by the President at the start of his term. Decisions within the Commission are taken in private and, if necessary, by simple majority vote.

The functions of the Commission are summarised as being those of initiative, supervision and implementation. It has the specific right to propose legislation to the Council, to implement the Council's decisions and generally to see that the legislation and other provisions laid down by the treaties are carried out. Under its direct control is a staff of European civil servants who, like the Commissioners, owe allegiance to the Community alone, even though leading officials are usually drawn from national civil services.

The Commission, whose members are mostly politicians, represents the governing cabinet, though its President cannot be compared to a prime minister. He neither selects nor decides alone on the functions of his fellow commissioners. He cannot dismiss them either. The Commission as a whole is answerable to the European Parliament, who can censure and dismiss it, a power never yet exercised.

The Maastricht Treaty has instituted some reforms affecting the Commission. As from January 1995 the Commission will be appointed for five years, a term coinciding in length with that of the European Parliament, though starting some six months after the parliamentary elections. Member governments will be obliged to consult the Parliament before nominating the President of the Commission who, in turn, will have to be consulted on the nomination of his fellow commissioners. Once nominated, the whole Commission will have to gain a vote of approval by the European Parliament. There is also a provision which would allow the number of commissioners to be altered, as long as it includes at least one commissioner from each member state. This potential change may well be applied to an enlarged Community in which the number of commissioners could be reduced to one only per country.

The importance of these reforms lies in two aspects. The Commission would become much more directly accountable to the European Parliament. The President's involvement in the appointment of, and presumably the allocation of functions to, his fellow commissioners would enhance his powers and status. To the public at large, however, the Commission would continue to present its current shadowy and rather faceless image.

From time to time, proposals have been put forward by European statesmen for the election of a President of the European Union to enhance its public image and the democratic legitimacy of its government. One possible way of achieving this objective would be through the direct election of the President of the Commission by direct suffrage, without necessarily increasing his powers. This would, at one stroke, focus public attention on the Union and raise public perception of the Commission to the level comparable to that of, say, the French presidency. If his election were held at the same time as those of the European Parliament it would no doubt increase public participation in European elections from their currently low levels. In line with the American example, a vice-president, elected on the same ticket, could be the President of the Parliament. Another vice-president, elected to act as the permanent chairman of the Council of Ministers would also become more logical if the Community is substantially enlarged.

THE COUNCIL

While the Commission represents the general European interest, the Council of Ministers brings to bear the interests of the member states on the decision-making process. The Council consists of representatives from each of the member states, with its meetings attended by at least one commissioner. The membership of the Council is, however, constantly changing, depending on the subject under discussion. Thus, finance ministers deal with the budget, agricultural ministers with the CAP and industrial ministers with matters related to industry. Foreign Ministers meet at least once a month in a General Affairs Council which, apart from foreign affairs, coordinates the work of the specialist Councils.

The principal legislature in the Community is the Council, to whom proposals for new laws, known as directives or regulations, are submitted by the Commission. Subject to opinions which have to be sought from the European Parliament, and often from the Economic and Social Committee, it is the Council that enacts the legislation. Contrary to practice in most parliamentary democracies, the Council debates and enacts the laws behind closed doors, although the Edinburgh Council agreed to open up some Council meetings to the media and publish voting figures on legislation decided by a qualified majority vote.

Under the Rome Treaty most decisions were ultimately supposed to be reached by qualified majority (now fifty-four votes out of seventy-six). Only a limited range of issues of major importance required unanimous agreement. The so-called Luxembourg compromise, reached in 1966, led to the practical suspension of all majority voting. If unanimity was not obtainable, issues were either dropped or allowed to lie on the table, often for years on end. The effect was to stultify progress and subordinate Community interests to those of individual member states.

For years many urgent reforms could not be effected. Where decisions were taken they tended to be at the lowest common denominator. Compromises reflected bargains between individual states, where one government might give way on issues on which it was not convinced in exchange for concessions on often quite unrelated matters. This process of 'log-rolling' may have satisfied some national interests but, inevitably, at the expense of the common good. The most notorious example of this practice has been the handling of the Common Agricultural Policy, where log-rolling led to massive and costly over-production, eating up for years up to three-quarters of the Community budget.

An examination of most criticisms levelled at the European Community over the years shows that responsibility for failure to make progress, for botched decisions, for delay and procrastination, and even for mismanagement resulting from flawed legislation lies with national governments and their representatives in the Community institutions. The habit of taking decisions only by unanimous agreement bred an attitude of mind that always put the national and even local parochial interest before that of the Community. On many occasions junior national civil servants vetoed consideration of minor legislative changes on the grounds that their government or minister would not approve.

Finally, feeling grew that to end the stagnation and to meet the challenges in the world at large, majority voting would have to return. And so the Treaty was amended by the Single European Act to reduce substantially issues on which unanimous agreement was required. On other issues, for which the treaties so provide, if agreement could not be reached, majority voting would actually be applied.

Since a proposal can be blocked by twenty-three votes out of seventy-six, only three large states acting together, or two large states with one small one (excepting Luxembourg) can block adoption. It would require at least five of the smaller states (with five votes each or less) to do so. The remarkable progress actually achieved towards the enactment of nearly 300 legislative proposals needed to create the single market is the best evidence of the benefits of abandoning the principle of unanimity. The mere threat of being outvoted is often quite enough to push governments towards compromise.

The Maastricht Treaty has taken majority voting further. Unanimity in the Council is retained for only a minority of important matters. These include the appointments to the Commission, Court of Justice, Court of Auditors and the Executive Board of the proposed European Central Bank, as well as decisions on the accession of new states and conclusion of association agreements. Unanimity is also required for the raising of the ceiling for Community taxes and for amendments to the treaties. Within the Community framework, (that is, excluding foreign and security policy, justice and home affairs), majority voting now applies to most matters except for decisions of a constitutional nature, that is, extensions of the Community's competences beyond those already defined in the Treaty.

The Council operates under a rotating presidency. Each member state takes turns for a six-month period and its representatives chair Council meetings. The function of the presidency should be to steer the Council towards agreement on as many as possible of the issues presented by the Commission. Foreign Ministers are designated Presidents of the Council during their country's term of presidency.

The work of the Council is prepared and assisted by large national delegations based in Brussels, headed by Permanent Representatives with status and rank of senior ambassadors. The committee of permanent representatives, called COREPER, meets weekly and tries to reach agreement on proposals submitted by the Commission. Proposals agreed are usually adopted by the appropriate Council without further debate. Controversial issues are left to the Councils to resolve. The final arbiter in cases where the Council has been unable to reach agreement is the summit meeting of the European Council.

The European Council of the Heads of State and of Governments, first launched on a regular basis in 1974, now meets at least once during the six months' term of the presidency of the Council, held in turn by each member state. Its function is to take decisions that the Council of Ministers has been unable to reach. It decides on treaty amendments and other important steps in developing the Community. Over the years it has come to play a central role in steering the Community towards the European Union.

Sir Michael Butler, a former British Permanent Representative, in his book *Europe: More than a Continent*, published in 1986, summarised the functions of the Council in the following terms: 'In one sense, COREPER and the Council together are a forum for a permanent negotiation between member governments on a wide range of issues simultaneously. In another, they are the legislature of the Community. In a third, they are the senior board of directors taking many of the day to day decisions on its policies' (Butler 1986).

During the long period between 1966 and 1985, when most decisions by the Council depended on unanimous agreement or consensus, the originally envisaged balance of power between Community institutions had become distorted. The Council became the dominant institution with the Commission increasingly relegated to the function of civil servants, even though it retained the exclusive right to propose legislation. It is not surprising, therefore, that European issues and concerns were subordinated to national interests and the Community slowly ground to a halt. The adoption of the Single European Act and the Maastricht Treaty, with majority voting on most issues covered by them, enables the distribution of powers between Community institutions to be brought back into balance.

The day-to-day management and conduct of Community affairs will increasingly revert to the Commission. The question arises, however, whether the rotating presidency of the Council is really the most efficient way to run the Community's legislative programme. Six months of the presidency is too short to prepare the legislative programme and shepherd it through. Too much is really expected of national civil servants who only once every six years have to take initiatives and manage the conduct of the Council. The lack of continuity is a major handicap in the efficient conduct of Community affairs. This weakness will grow as the Community is further enlarged.

The question is whether one could not arrive at a longer or

even more permanent leadership of the Council and, at the same time, link relations between Community institutions more closely. One possible suggestion would be to appoint or elect the President of the Council to hold office for the duration of the life of the Commission and Parliament. A senior European statesman commanding general respect among governments might be acceptable as the permanent chairman, who would furthermore head the permanent secretariat of the Council. He could stand as one of the two vice-presidents of the Union on the ticket of an elected President of the Commission, suggested above.

Under this system the presidents of the Community's three principal institutions would be a team, committed to the same overall programme for which they would have obtained a general mandate directly from the citizens of the Community. Of course the detailed programmes of legislation and the conduct of Community affairs would continue to be accountable to and require the approval of the Council and Parliament.

THE PARLIAMENT

This leads us to the consideration of the balance of powers between the Council and Parliament. The European Parliament succeeded a nominated Assembly of national parliamentarians which, under the various treaties, was largely confined to an advisory role. It became directly elected in 1979 and consisted of 518 full-time members, whose powers have, however, increased only very slowly. From 1994 the numbers will have been further increased to 567, largely to accommodate the unified Germany and to enlarge slightly the representation of the larger member states.

It has the right to dismiss the Commission by a vote of censure, but cannot censure individual commissioners. On budgetary matters it shares powers with the Council and agreement between the institutions is necessary for the budget to be adopted. The legislative role of the Parliament remains essentially advisory, though the Council cannot enact legislation without first consulting the Parliament. Theoretically, this could have allowed the Parliament to block legislation it did not like. However, under the Single Act and the Maastricht Treaty these powers have now been extended: on most issues covered by them, the Parliament can now amend or reject legislation proposed by the Council. In such an event, the Council has to act by unanimity if it wishes to override the Parliament's objections. As a result, on a number of specified issues, the two institutions have now moved closer towards a process of co-decision over legislation.

A significant gap still exists regarding the democratic account-ability of the Community to its citizens, compared with that enjoyed in relation to their elected national, regional and local governments. Although the European Parliament is directly elected, its powers certainly do not match those of national parliaments. The Council, which is still the principal legislative organ of the Community, cannot be collectively held accountable for its actions.

As long as Council decisions required unanimous agreement, each minister could, theoretically, be held answerable for his decisions in his national parliament. Once majority voting ap-plies, especially behind closed doors, no individual minister can be personally held accountable. And the collective decisions of the Council cannot be subjected to scrutiny by the individual twelve national parliaments – to whom the Council is not consti-tutionally responsible.

If the Community's actions and decisions are to retain demo-cratic legitimacy, then the directly elected European Parliament must acquire legislative powers equal to those of the Council. Co-decision, now exercised over a few specified issues, should be extended to the whole field of Community action.

OTHER INSTITUTIONS

One of the important remaining institutions of the Community is the Court of Justice, based in Luxembourg, whose thirteen judges and six advocates-general ensure that Community law is applied and obeyed. Then there is the Court of Auditors, which oversees the accounts of all Community institutions and bodies set up by them. There is an Economic and Social Committee, a purely advisory body which must, however, be consulted by the Commission and Council over a wide range of issues. It consists of three interest groups, generally described as the social part-ners. The first group represents employers, the second workers and the third various interests including consumers, farmers, the self-employed, academics, etc. Its members, nominated by gov-ernments, are appointed for renewable four-year terms. Finally, under the Maastricht Treaty, a further consultative body set up is the Committee of the Regions of 189 members, appointed by the Council for four-year terms. Its powers correspond to those of the Economic and Social Committee.

A FEDERAL UNION

The changes introduced in the Maastricht Treaty have brought the Community closer to becoming a federal union. Once the Economic and Monetary Union, with a single currency under the control of the European Central Bank, is achieved, the Union will have acquired federal powers. The principle of subsidiarity has reinforced its federal nature by defining the distribution of powers between the European and national levels of government. If the Parliament acquires full powers of codecision with the Council it will become the federal legislature, and the Commission, in effect elected and answerable to the Parliament, will emerge as the executive or federal government of the Union. But to complete the federation it will need to incorporate within its institutional structure foreign policy, defence, justice and home affairs, now conducted on an intergovernmental basis under the Treaty.

Finally, to give the federation life and meaning for its citizens will require a written and intelligible constitution. This will have to include a detailed description of the aims of the federation and of its institutions, and a definition of the federal competences and those remaining with member states and sub-national tiers of government. It should embody a charter of citizens' rights, on the lines described in Chapter 5. It will need a provision for amending the constitution. At present, treaty amendments require unanimous agreement of member states and, after Maastricht, the consent of the European Parliament. As the Community is further enlarged to perhaps double its membership, unanimity for constitutional amendments could prevent necessary changes and stop further progress. Approval by, say, threequarters of the number of member states might become acceptable if this were coupled with confirmation in a popular vote or referendum of the Union's citizens.

Whether referenda should be used for constitutional changes has been an issue of major contention during the ratification debates of the Maastricht Treaty. Four referenda were actually

held: one each in France and Ireland, two in Denmark, the
second reversing the decision of the first. In Britain in particular
there was much agitation by Maastricht's opponents for a referendum on the lines conducted in 1975 on British membership of
the Community. The arguments against this were advanced by
those who claimed that representative democracy exercised by
elected parliamentarians should suffice. However, the commitment of all political parties to the parliamentary ratification, even
with substantial minorities among their ranks against it, seemed
to make whipped decisions unfair. With cross-party divisions on
this issue, a free vote in Parliament might have been preferable,
but the general public would still not have been involved, particularly as in the preceding general election they had no party
choice on this issue.

One of the arguments against decisions being made through
a referendum is that votes are frequently cast on the basis of
unconnected issues, such as dislike of the ruling government.
Furthermore, wise decisions are not very likely to come from
voters who are demonstrably ill-informed on the substance of the
issues posed by a referendum. That is why the public needs to be
constantly well-informed about the Community, its activities and
all it stands for. Indeed, opinion polls have shown during the
Maastricht ratification debates throughout the Community that
the public lacked information and was resentful of governments
and parliaments for taking such major decisions over their heads
and without formal consultation.

If the European federation is to be well understood and become acceptable to its citizens, the adoption of its constitution
and any amendments to it must be subjected to a lengthy and
comprehensive public debate. But to acquire full legitimacy
major constitutional changes should be taken by a majority vote
in a referendum among all the citizens of the federation.

Chapter 7

One Europe

The collapse of the Soviet empire and its splintering into a large number of independent democratic states operating social market economies has presented the European Community with a massive challenge. The opportunity is to try and unite the whole of our continent and thus banish for ever war between its states, in the way in which the Community has succeeded for its own membership. The dangers of failure, so dramatically demonstrated in former Yugoslavia, is that large parts of the continent could be plunged into internecine wars and ultimately threaten the very survival of the European Community itself.

The collapse in the East came about largely as a result of the economic failure of the Soviet Union and its rigid command system to keep up with the successes of the market-oriented economies in the West. To reverse the ever growing gap between East and West, Mikhail Gorbachev, elected General Secretary of the Soviet communist party in 1985, tried to reform the communist system. At the same time he resolved to reduce the USSR's worldwide commitments and stop the arms race, the costs of which were no longer sustainable.

THE END OF THE SOVIET UNION

The changes in Soviet policy had the most dramatic consequences. Soviet troops were withdrawn from Afghanistan, ending the costly military invasion. Subservient communist governments in satellite countries in Central and Eastern Europe collapsed one after another and their democratic successors reasserted their independence from the big brother in the East. The Warsaw Pact was dissolved, Soviet troops were progressively withdrawn and

Comecon, the economic institution set up to regulate trade and investment between the countries of the Soviet empire, disappeared without trace. Within the Soviet Union itself, individual republics tried to establish greater autonomy, while efforts were being made to reform the economic system. The reforms undermined the monopoly of power of the communist party and this, in the end, led to a coup against Gorbachev in 1991 by the very people he had chosen to help him govern the country. Although the coup failed after three days, Gorbachev was soon forced to resign and power was assumed by Boris Yeltsin, the newly elected President of the Russian Federation.

The abortive coup precipitated the end of communist rule, with the party being banned in Russia and replaced in most of the other republics by parties under new names, though often under the same leadership. In rejecting the monopoly of the communist party and its command economy, the centralised union started falling apart. An attempt to retain it within the so-called Commonwealth of Independent States soon collapsed, and one by one the fifteen republics proclaimed their sovereignty and independence from Moscow. Russia, itself a federation of several republics and autonomous regions, continues to struggle to retain its cohesiveness, but stresses within it may well lead to its further dissolution. Nationalist movements have sprung up in most republics, leading to tensions and conflicts between ethnic groups within individual countries and often between them. Some twenty-five million Russians have found themselves as minorities in neighbouring countries, adding tensions to relations between them. The faltering attempts to replace the state-controlled economic system by a market-oriented one have led to massive upheavals, dramatic reductions in living standards, the collapse of the social security system, all bringing with them the threat of widespread social unrest and chaos.

CENTRAL AND EASTERN EUROPE

Soviet acquiescence in the independence of its former satellites on its western borders led rapidly to the collapse of the communist governments of these countries in 1989 and 1990. The first non-communist government emerged in Poland, when candidates nominated by the *Solidarność* movement won, in the June 1989 general elections, 99 per cent of the seats in the upper house and practically all the freely contested seats in the lower house. Reserving for themselves and their coalition allies 65 per cent of the seats in the lower house the communists hoped to retain power. But they were abandoned by their coalition partners who, by switching support to *Solidarność*, enabled the latter to form a new government. At the start of 1990 it introduced revolutionary economic and monetary changes aimed at a rapid transformation of the command system into a market economy. It brought spectacular results. Inflation running at some 80 per cent in January dropped to single figures within three months. The Polish currency became fully convertible, and goods not seen for decades became readily available, though at much higher prices. On paper, living standards fell by one-third or more, but in reality the drop was less dramatic. Previously there was plenty of money about but nothing to buy for it. The return to a market-based economy meant that there were now goods available to match the purchasing power of the population. Unemployment, however, grew and so have new inequalities between 'haves' and 'have-nots', creating social strains, strikes and unrest among the less favoured sectors such as the miners and farmers.

Poland has also suffered from political instability. Its first *Solidarność* government came into conflict with its founder and leader Lech Walesa after he had been elected President in December 1990. The parliamentary elections, which followed in 1991, resulted in an assembly of 29 parties, with the largest gaining less than 15 per cent of seats. Consecutive coalition governments remained unstable until July 1992, when a government coalition of seven political parties under its prime minister Hanna Suchocka managed to re-establish a semblance of political stability.

Since then economic reforms, including the speeding up of privatisation, the modernisation of the agricultural sector and the raising of the efficiency in the state sector have shown results. By 1992 economic decline was arrested and modest growth in GNP has reappeared. Foreign trade with the West has grown rapidly, showing a 20 per cent increase in 1992 over the previous year, which more than compensated for the loss of trade with the former Soviet Union.

Poland's biggest problem remains with the vast foreign debts incurred by the previous regime. Interest and capital repayments have, however, been substantially alleviated and postponed by the western creditors. Provided Poland continues its progress towards an efficient market economy, remains open to foreign trade and investment and controls its budget deficit, the heavy debts might in time cease to pose a threat to the country's future prosperity.

Hungarian reforms designed to move towards a market-based economy started much earlier than in Poland, but failure by the communist government to relinquish control over the main sectors of the economy, or to allow large enterprises to meet the full force of competition, stifled earlier improvements. Economic decline resulted in pressure for political change and led to the toppling of Janos Kadar, the communist leader of the country, installed by the Russians after the abortive 1956 revolution. After intensive internal debate and a number of governmental changes, the general elections held in May 1990 resulted in the defeat of the communists and the emergence of a non-communist coalition government, determined to cut all links with the previous regime. While the Polish shock remedies had been rejected, economic reforms towards a full market system are moving apace. The Hungarian florint, made convertible, has become the region's hard currency and has attracted big foreign investments. Exports have grown rapidly: in 1992 by some 20 per cent over the previous year.

Politically, however, growth of nationalism has been fuelled by concern over the fate of the large Hungarian minorities living in neighbouring Slovakia, Romania, the Ukraine and in Serbia's province of Vojvodina. This has raised fears in those countries about possible Hungarian territorial claims, fuelled by Hungarian premier Joszef Antall who, on taking office, declared himself leader of all Hungarians, wherever they might live. He did, however, state that Hungary would not pursue the redrawing of Europe's frontiers provided universal standards for the protection of ethnic minorities were adopted in the region – a vain aspiration at present in the light of the ethnic cleansing in former Yugoslavia.

The revolution in Czechoslovakia was bloodless. The student-led protests in Prague brought about the rapid collapse of the government and its voluntary acceptance of non-communists into leading government positions. The communist-dominated parliament elected the dissident playwright Václav Havel as president only a few months after his release from jail. The June 1990 elections resulted in a massive victory for the non-communist parties. A new coalition government headed by an ex-communist introduced economic reforms at a steady pace. A relatively low level of foreign indebtedness and the experience of a rather successful industrial economy before the Second World War promises a manageable conversion into a full market economy. Withdrawal of Soviet troops was negotiated and the government has championed a new system of common security in Europe to replace the Warsaw Pact.

The general election of June 1992 delivered a major shock to the Czechoslovak federal republic, first established more than seventy years ago after the First World War. A nationalist Movement for Democratic Slovakia under Vladimir Meciar sought greater Slovak sovereignty within the federation. The new Czech premier Václav Klaus, heading a right-wing government, failed to reach agreement with the Slovaks. In its absence they agreed to split the federation into two separate sovereign states which came into effect on 1 January 1993. The Czech Republic, economically more advanced and diversified, introduced radical reforms which have brought it much foreign investment and good export prospects. Already in 1992 Czechoslovakia's exports, largely generated in its Czech part, rose by 23 per cent over the previous year.

Slovakia, hitherto largely dependent on arms production and other heavy industries, faces major economic difficulties. Privatisation of the large state-owned enterprises is difficult and much less foreign investment has been attracted. With some 600,000 ethnic Hungarians, representing 12 per cent of Slovakia's population, as well as a large normadic gypsy population, the nationalist government failed to make any provisions for the protection of the rights of ethnic minorities, adding to tensions with neighbouring Hungary. These had already been seriously affected by the dispute between the two countries over the diversion of the Danube river and its ecologically damaging proposed dam. In spite of these tensions the dissolution of Czechoslovakia was peacefully achieved and relations with other neighbours remain tolerable.

In contrast, the Romanian revolution at the end of 1989 was far from peaceful. The execution of the dictator Ceausescu and his wife by the army, which refused to suppress the anti-government demonstrations that erupted throughout the country, did not, however, lead to the rejection of the communists. Those who gained power had all been members of the previous regime and have continued the old methods of suppressing democratic protest. The May 1990 general elections did not follow Polish, Hungarian or Czechoslovak examples. The non-communist parties, harassed by government-backed forces, failed to overturn the communist majority which under a new name, the National Salvation Front, won 66 per cent of the seats, while its leader, Ion Illiescu, was elected president with 85 per cent of the vote. Although practically free from foreign debt, the economy is at a very low ebb, poverty is widespread and living standards wretched. Social protest and ethnic unrest between Romanians and the large Hungarian minority in Transylvania continues to erupt and threatens both internal stability and relations with neighbouring Hungary.

Change in Bulgaria has not been as dramatic as in the rest of Eastern Europe. The communist dictator Todor Zhivkov was deposed by his party in November 1989 after 35 years of rule. The party changed its name and the new leaders, although they had held senior positions in the old regime, declared themselves its opponents, in favour of multi-party democracy and a market economy. In the June 1990 elections they won nearly half of the votes, well ahead of their nearest non-communist rivals. Whereas in other Eastern European countries communists were regarded as collaborators of a hated foreign power, Bulgarians have always looked to their Russian Slav brothers for support against the Turks, and there were no Soviet troops in Bulgaria. Thus communism and nationalism were not incompatible and the deeply traditional rural population distrusted the less experienced city-based intellectuals standing for the opposition. Gradual economic change is the order of the day.

The collapse of authoritarian communist regimes all around them have had far-reaching effect on the cohesiveness and stability of the Yugoslav federation. Not tied to the Soviet block since the late 1940s, successive Yugoslav communist governments, starting with Tito in the 1960s, introduced reforms aimed at decentralising the command economy and moving towards a socialist market system that has not really worked. After Tito's death the highly centralised political system at federal level began to loosen and the constituent republics sought ever greater autonomy. Internal economic failure and the collapse of communist systems elsewhere finally precipitated separatist tendencies. Slovenia, with the highest living standards, threatened to leave the federation and to apply for European Community membership. Croatia, after electing a non-communist government in 1990, wanted to follow Slovenia's example. The largest republic, Serbia, tried to assert its dominance over the semi-autonomous province of Kosovo with its almost entirely Albanian population. The Serbs, forming the largest ethnic group within the federation, had ambitions to extend their influence over the whole country.

The resulting differences finally led to a vicious civil war and the dissolution of the Yugoslav federation. Slovenia and Croatia gained their independence and international recognition, though the latter suffered the loss of nearly one-third of its territory to occupation by Serb irregulars, backed by the Serbian-controlled former Yugoslav armed forces. A fragile ceasefire, policed by United Nations troops, followed, though with little promise of permanent peace. Bosnia's fate was much worse. The country was torn apart by a vicious civil war between the Muslim majority, representing more than 40 per cent of the population and its two ethnic minorities of Serbs and Croats. The brutality of the war has led to hundreds of thousands of casualties and millions of refugees, ejected through ethnic cleansing by the irregular partisans, armed and backed by Serbia and Croatia respectively. Media coverage of the holocaust finally moved the international community to intervene, first to bring humanitarian aid and then to sponsor an uneasy ceasefire which, if finally achieved, will require years of international policing before an acceptable peace settlement is reached.

Great instability remains in Serbia's province of Kosovo, 90 per cent of whose population is Albanian, but claimed by the Serbs as their ancient inalienable territory. Oppression of ethnic Albanians has raised major tensions with the newly emerged democratic Albania, whose own hope is one day to reunite their peoples in a greater Albania. This matches Serbia's own intentions to replace the former Yugoslavia with a greater Serbia. While the new republic of Montenegro remains linked with the Serbs, Macedonia in the south has declared its independence. This is fiercely contested by the Greeks, who assert that the usurpation by the new state of the name 'Macedonia' implies its territorial claim upon Northern Greece, inhabited by the descendants of ancient Macedonia.

Thus the Balkans remain a powder keg which could at any time explode, engulfing the whole region in wars reminiscent of those that followed the collapse of the Ottoman empire and led to the First World War at the beginning of this century. Instability in south-eastern Europe is in some ways a mirror-image of the instability within the former Soviet Union itself. From a tightly and centrally controlled single party command economy, political and economic reforms aimed at devolving power have suddenly lifted the lid off previously suppressed separatist national and ethnic ambitions of a wide mix of races, nationalities, languages, cultures and religions. The failure, hitherto, of the economic reforms and the continuing fall in living standards in many of the countries are increasing the strains. Political and social unrest, including armed conflicts in some of the Central Asian republics, are seriously threatening overall peace in that region also.

GERMAN UNIFICATION

The collapse of the communist regime in eastern Germany carried, however, the most immediate consequences for the European Community. The dismantling of the Berlin Wall was a signal for the end of a divided Germany. Once the communists were defeated in the March 1990 elections there was no further reason to maintain the existence of a separate German state in the east. Unification, as rapidly as possible, became the goal of all political forces in both Germanies. Monetary union in July 1990 was quickly followed by a full political merger in October. The democratic transformation of the eastern German economy, financed by the west Germans, was to be painful for the hundreds of thousands losing their jobs. But it was rapid and could provide a pattern and example to other Central and Eastern European countries trying to become market economies themselves.

Initial reactions of Germany's western allies to the prospects of unification were anxious and hesitant. Countries within the Warsaw Pact, with the Second World War still in mind, were fearful and hostile at first. The prospects were of a united Germany of some eighty million inhabitants, economically the most successful and prosperous country in Europe, becoming the preponderant power on the continent. Genuine fears were expressed by some, in the west as well as in the east, that what Germany had failed to achieve by force of arms under Hitler, she would be able to secure by economic domination. A united, sovereign, independent and powerful Germany in the centre of Europe seemed to pose a renewed threat which its divided status over the previous forty years had effectively removed.

History has, however, moved on. The Federal Republic is a founder member of the European Community. It has always been one of the strongest protagonists of the Community's transformation into a European federation, and this objective is actually spelt out in the German constitution. The French, mindful of their history of past wars and conflicts with the Germans, were the first to react. They recognised that, even within the existing Community, a united Germany could become the dominant partner, dictating its future course and development. That is why French President Mitterrand called for the speeding up of progress towards a full economic and political union within which national sovereignties were pooled and no single country could impose its will. The Germans responded enthusiastically and support for Mitterrand's call followed from most other Community countries. As a consequence, the European Council of heads of governments agreed, in April 1990, to convene an intergovernmental conference on Political Union at the end of the year, to be held in parallel with the one aimed at Economic and Monetary Union. Thus German unification provided the principal and a powerful spur for faster progress to full European Union, envisaged in the Maastricht Treaty.

THE NEXT ENLARGEMENT

The contrast between the relative prosperity of the European Community and the turbulence, economic misery and political instability in the formerly communist part of our continent has made the Community a powerful pole of attraction. The ending of the East–West divide and its military confrontation has, furthermore, removed much of the hesitation of neutral countries in Europe about becoming more closely associated with the Community.

The countries of the European Free Trade Association (EFTA), consisting of Austria, Finland, Iceland, Liechtenstein, Norway, Sweden and Switzerland, have enjoyed free trade agreements with the European Community, negotiated after its founder members Britain, Denmark and Ireland joined the Community in

1973. When the Single European Act was negotiated, fears were expressed by the EFTA countries that they might be at a disadvantage in their economic relations with the emerging single European internal market. To allay these fears, negotiations between the Community and EFTA resulted in an agreement in February 1992 to create a common European Economic Area (EEA). The former free trade agreements abolished customs duties and quantitative restrictions in trade and industrial goods. The EEA agreement removed other trade barriers and added the freedom of movement for people, services and capital. This was achieved by the EFTA countries' adopting past Community legislation – the so-called *acquis communautaire*, subject to specific adaptations, transitional periods and a few derogations. Future Community legislation will be subject to consultation with the EFTA countries, but without their right to vote on it.

The EEA agreement was due to come into force on 1 January 1993, after ratification. However, the Swiss electorate rejected the agreement narrowly in a referendum at the end of 1992. The agreement had, therefore, to be adjusted to exclude Switzerland from its provisions, though that country will continue to enjoy free trade with her EFTA partners and the Community on the basis that applied before the establishment of the EEA.

The exclusion of EFTA countries, under the EEA, from participation in voting on Community laws affecting them, persuaded a majority of them to seek full Community membership. The end of the East–West confrontation largely removed the reservations of the neutral Austrians, Finns, Swedes and Swiss about joining the Community. The Austrians applied in July 1989. Sweden followed in June 1991. Then, in 1992, Finland applied in March, Switzerland in May and Norway in November. Having, however, lost the referendum on joining the EEA, Switzerland is unlikely, for the time being, to pursue full membership of the Community.

Opinions given by the Commission on the applications have all been favourable, subject to the acceptance by the applicants of the full *acquis communautaire*, the aims and objectives of the Community and all the provisions of the Maastricht Treaty. The applicants have declared their readiness to accept these, though some of them are hoping that, with regard to defence integration envisaged under Maastricht, they will be able to negotiate derogations similar to those enjoyed by Ireland and Denmark. Negotiations with Austria, Finland and Sweden started at the beginning of 1992 and the Norwegians joined them a few months later. Following the detailed negotiations on the EEA, most of the issues concerning full membership had already been settled and little has remained to be resolved. Ratification, however, presents more of a problem. Referenda will have to be conducted in the applicant countries under their constitutions. Nevertheless, after the successful second Danish referendum, the obstacles are likely to be overcome in most, if not all the countries. The Community is thus set to be enlarged by up to sixteen members by the end of 1995 at the latest.

ENLARGEMENT TO THE SOUTH

When Turkey negotiated its association agreement with the Community in 1963, possible full membership was envisaged by 1997, with a customs union being established in 1995. In 1987 Turkey submitted a formal application for membership, but the European Commission, in an opinion issued at the end of 1989, declared that neither Turkey nor the Community were yet fit and ready to open enlargement negotiations. The Commission's principal reservations were the size of Turkey, its rapidly growing population, already in excess of sixty million, its weak economy and political considerations. It judged that Turkey, with lower living standards than the Community's poorest members and large parts at third-world levels of development, would be unable to handle the economic adjustment problems of accession. Its political institutions were also seen as not sufficiently developed, and there were serious concerns about Turkey's human rights record, particularly in relation to their very large Kurdish minority. Finally, the conflict between Turkey and Greece over Cyprus made it unlikely that accession would receive the unanimous agreement of all the Community members required under the treaties.

Since then, however, the Middle East crisis and the independence of the central Asian republics of the former Soviet Union have made Turkey's role pivotal in the region. Growing Muslim fundamentalism has not affected Turkey, a secular state in which religion plays no greater role than in Christian Europe. The Turkic-speaking Asian republics look upon Turkey as their model, while Turkey's influence upon Middle Eastern developments could make a major contribution to peace and stability in the region. Turkey continues, however, to look towards Europe and Community membership as its goal, which, if thwarted, could undermine Turkish democracy and secularism. Denial of Turkey's European ambitions would be a bitter blow to a founder of the Council of Europe in 1949 and a loyal member of the North Atlantic Treaty Organisation (NATO) since its inception. The Community's own interests in extending its influence and safe-guarding the stability of southeastern Europe, the Middle East and the Central Asian republics would be well served by Turkey's accession. A firm commitment to consider Turkey's membership has become desirable, subject to a specified transition period during which its economy and political institutions would be helped to undergo adjustments enabling Turkey to accept the responsibilities of membership.

The outstanding problem is Turkish military intervention to protect the Turkish Cypriots in Northern Cyprus. A commitment to help achieve the reunification of that country in a federation of autonomous regions could remove the main Greek objections to Turkish membership of the Community. It would at the same time allow Cyprus also to join. Cyprus negotiated an association agreement with the Community in 1972. A full customs union is to be achieved by 1997. In 1990 the Greek Cypriot government applied for full membership, but meaningful negotiations would have to await the reunification of the island.

Malta is another candidate. It has an association agreement with the Community, first negotiated in 1970 and repeatedly extended, leading up to an eventual customs union. The Maltese government applied for full Community membership in 1990 and its accession should not present major difficulties. With a popu-lation of some 300,000 it equals that of Luxembourg: 75 per cent of its trade is with the Community and its per capita income is higher that that of Greece and Portugal. Malta's hope is that its membership might be considered alongside that of the EFTA applicants.

ENLARGEMENT TO THE EAST

Then there are the countries of Central and Eastern Europe that have abandoned the communist system and are trying rapidly to convert themselves into full market economies. Although they have successfully detached themselves from dictation by Moscow and re-established their political independence, they are most anxious to develop the closest economic relations with their western neighbours, and with the European Community in particular. They are fully aware that, without substantial help from and cooperation with the West, their economic transformation will be difficult to achieve – with internal social tensions and conflicts threatening the very survival of their new pluralist democratic political systems.

Recognising the dangers but also the opportunities in the East, the West including the USA entrusted the European Community with channelling help to the new democracies in the East. The European Bank for Reconstruction and Development (EBRD) with an initial membership of some forty countries was established for this purpose. It is, however, becoming increasingly clear that much more needs to be done if the transformation of Central and Eastern European countries into pluralist democratic market economies is not to fail. The post-war American Marshall Plan was one example of how shattered economies in Europe were helped to help themselves rebuild their prosperity. The current experience of the transformation of the east German economy within a united Germany could be even more relevant. The nature and scale of the reforms needed are similar and the German example could act as a guide in mapping out the type of help needed by the rest of Central and Eastern Europe. Quite apart from the economic benefits likely to flow back ultimately to the donors of an imaginative and generous programme of help, which would create vast new markets for their exports, a rapid and successful transition of the economies of the recipients would safeguard democracy. Failure risks the resurgence of extreme nationalism, social and ethnic unrest, the re-establishment of authoritarian regimes and threats to stability and peace in Europe.

Looking beyond the economic transformation of their countries, most of the governments involved have declared their interest in participating in the process of European cooperation and integration. They have applied to join the Council of Europe, and most of them, including the former Soviet republics, have either been accepted or accorded observer status in anticipation of full membership, once they have adopted fully democratic pluralist political systems.

Furthermore, the majority of the Central and Eastern European countries have declared their intention to seek full membership of the European Community once their economies have been reformed and reached a level enabling them to accept its rules and obligations.

The political pull of integration within the emerging European Union has, paradoxically, an even greater attraction for the Central and Eastern European countries. Although they have succeeded in re-establishing their independence and sovereignty by breaking away from the Moscow-dominated Soviet empire, they are aware that in our rapidly shrinking world total political and economic independence is no longer relevant or possible. Furthermore, like the EFTA countries, they can also see that only full participation within the European Community would ensure an effective say and share in decisions, to which they will increasingly become subject as long as they remain outside the Community. The emerging European federation, in which decisions are shared for some matters but national autonomy is reserved for most other issues, and in which distinct cultural identities are fully guaranteed and maintained, offers an attractive alternative to the uncertainties of unfettered national sovereignty that would exclude them from an increasingly interdependent world.

Responding to them, the European Community first introduced the so-called PHARE programme of aid to Poland and Hungary, later extended to other Central and East European countries. Then it negotiated special association agreements called Europe Agreements with Poland, Czechoslovakia, Hungary, Romania and Bulgaria. When peace has finally been secured in former Yugoslavia, similar agreements are likely to be negotiated with Slovenia and Croatia, who have also declared their wish to join the Community. In the case of other Eastern European countries less far-reaching trade and cooperation agreements have been concluded.

The Europe Agreements are designed to speed up development of trade and investment directed at economic restructuring and technological modernisation. While ultimately aiming at totally free trade, the agreements have been criticised for restricting access into the Community for agricultural products, textiles, clothing, iron and steel. Nor is free movement of workers envisaged. There is to be a political dialogue in which the associates are to be briefed on the Community's common foreign and security policies. This is rather one-sided and hardly represents the partnership that is ultimately supposed to lead to membership.

Firm expectations of full economic and political membership of the Community would provide these countries with a definite political objective. They need this clear perspective if they are to combat disruptive nationalist tendencies and risks to the survival of their still fragile democracies. The offer of full membership within a reasonable timescale would act as a powerful factor of political stability and a safeguard against any attempts at authoritarian alternatives that would prejudice their prospective membership of the Community.

It took seven years from the date of their application for Spain and Portugal to join the Community. With this lengthy transition as an example, is it not possible and indeed advisable for the Community to be much more positive? It should offer an assurance to those Central and Eastern European countries who wish to join that, subject to the necessary economic transformation and the maintenance of political pluralism, they would be admitted to membership of the Community within a specified number of years but not later than by the end of this century. Nothing would contribute more to the confidence of those countries, speed up internal reforms and safeguard their democracies than a clear goal within a defined timescale of full membership of the emerging European Union. If further economic adjustments were necessary, these could form part of transitional arrangements of appropriate length after a country joins.

RELATIONS WITH FORMER SOVIET REPUBLICS

Among the former members of the Soviet federation, the three Baltic states of Estonia, Latvia and Lithuania have managed to detach themselves from the Commonwealth of Independent States and have sought help from the West to transform their economies. Special relations have been forged with their Scandinavian neighbours. Ultimately, however, they would also wish to be considered for Community membership, which could become easier once the Scandinavian EFTA countries join.

Full European Community membership for the other CIS republics, and Russia in particular, even when they become fully democratic market economies, is not really within the realm of practical politics. The Soviet Union is a nuclear superpower with a population half that of the Community, with a landmass stretching from Eastern Europe right to the Pacific ocean. Its membership would totally change the nature of the Community and put into question the careful political and constitutional balance between its present medium-sized and small member countries. The likely enlargement of the Community after 1992 to the EFTA countries and further east which ultimately that might have to accommodate perhaps double its current membership, will require further institutional reforms, carefully conserving checks and balances between its members. These would be totally distorted by membership of a giant country of the size of Russia.

The future relationship with the former Soviet republics requires a different direction. The Community's interests lie in helping them to achieve internal reforms, leading to decentralised market economies and political freedoms. Such reforms will not only benefit their peoples, but should secure the reduction of international tensions, stimulate trade and foster closer cooperation with the rest of Europe.

A positive policy of help and cooperation from the West that brings tangible economic benefits to the republics will furthermore strengthen the hands of the present reformers and help their successors to prevent the system from slipping back into its bad old ways. Such a policy would need more than the benevolent cheering from the sidelines that has characterised most western reactions to their effort to reform.

The republics need to increase their trade with the West, particularly in technologically advanced goods, to help speed up the modernisation of their industries. The Russians have called for western enterprises to set up plants under joint venture agreements. There is a case for many more exchanges, including the training of management and technical personnel. Contacts like these, coupled with much greater cultural links, will increase knowledge and understanding and inevitably encourage a more open and pluralist society in those countries.

More needs to be done, however, if growing cooperation between East and West is not to be arrested, or even reversed by the toppling of the present democratic leaders and a return to more closed and repressive regimes. If future cooperation and the developing system of common security is to be assured, the Community's own origins might provide some signposts.

The principal motives of the founders of the Community were to make future wars between its member countries impossible. They achieved the objective by progressively integrating their economies, starting with the placing of the coal and steel industries under supranational control. The choice of coal and steel was designed to remove from national control basic industries which were then essential for military rearmament.

At the present crucial stage in Europe's history a similar imaginative leap forward could well provide safeguards for the mutual security for which both sides of our Continent so clearly yearn. Today it is coal, oil, gas and nuclear power that generate modern economies and fuel the armed forces. Already our common needs for energy transcend our divisions. In spite of past American opposition, Siberian gas now flows through pipelines into Western Europe and Polish coal generates some of our electricity. The use of fossil fuels has at the same time been responsible for much of the pollution that is threatening our environment. Nuclear energy poses other major threats, highlighted by the Chernobyl disaster and the almost insoluble problems of nuclear waste disposal.

Suppose that these primary sources of energy were to be brought under international control, with the aim of effecting their rational development and safe use for the whole of Europe, East and West; and that the conservation of our common environment, so much dependent on the methods of generating energy for industry and transport, were to be similarly controlled. An independent Energy and Environment Authority established on the basis of equality between the European Community, the former Soviet republics and any other interested European states, whose decisions were binding on all participants, would introduce a novel supranational element into Euro-Asian relations. Its existence and the acceptance of its rulings would generate trust and could lead to a rapid extension of economic cooperation with the republics.

The European Community's own early experience showed how the habit of working together, and growing interdependence, made it impossible for President de Gaulle to reverse the process when the French withdrew from the Community's Council of Ministers for several months in 1965. The benefits of membership proved too strong and persuaded him back to the negotiating table and, after the so-called Luxembourg compromise, to the continued development of the Community.

Were an East–West European Energy and Environment Authority to be established, is it not also likely that growing cooperation and interdependence would soon make the process irreversible? Mutual benefits would surely outweigh any arguments in favour of the re-erection of barriers and a renewal of confrontation, whoever happened to be in charge in national capitals. The trust generated could ultimately, as in Western Europe today, make military confrontation between individual countries or groups of them not only unnecessary but quite irrelevant.

Even if differing political and economic systems were to continue to divide us, such differences might in the long run be no greater or more threatening than existing linguistic or religious differences within our own countries. These may sometimes lead to quarrels or conflicts as in Belgium or in Northern Ireland but, however regrettable, they do not threaten our very survival. East–West interdependence might not remove all rivalries, but could well make obsolete all armed conflict between us in Europe and lead to a permanent system of common security.

Chapter 8

Global role

We live in a world that has shrunk in all except its purely physical dimensions. Not only are we instantly aware of major political, economic, social or physical events taking place anywhere in the world, but we are directly or indirectly affected by most of them. The very survival of humanity is at risk should a nuclear conflict ever break out. Parts of our planet could become uninhabitable for thousands of years in the event of major nuclear accidents, of which the Chernobyl disaster was such a terrible warning. Political and economic rivalries have precipitated two world wars this century. The cold war era of confrontation between the capitalist and communist camps could well have led to a third world war. Smaller and more local conflicts between countries provide a constant threat of spreading and drawing in others.

Economically we have become increasingly interdependent. Self-sufficiency is either a necessity confined to very poor and isolated communities, or a means of escape for groups of individuals nostalgically anxious to recreate economic and social conditions of allegedly happier and more primitive past societies that did not rely on the 'benefits' of technology and modern civilisation. For the rest of us, life is largely dependent upon outside sources of food, energy and raw materials.

Even Europe as a whole cannot subsist on its own resources. The European Community depends for most of its energy on imports of coal, gas and oil from countries in other parts the world. It is the biggest food importer, and most of the raw materials for its industries come from overseas. Uncontrolled exploitation and depletion of finite resources could eventually deprive our industries of the means to continue supplying our daily needs.

Large parts of our globe and indeed the whole of humanity could be damaged by ecological changes brought about by our own actions. Massive air, water and soil pollution, destroying our forests, poisoning our lakes and crops and crumbling our buildings, is with us already. Deforestation is the main cause of major flood disasters and the spread of barren deserts that in recent years have resulted in large-scale famines. Global warming, caused by carbon dioxide produced by the burning of coal, oil and gas, is a distinct possibility. Over the next two or three decades global temperatures could increase by 4.5 degrees Centigrade. This would raise ocean levels by some 1.4 metres and flood vast expanses of land. Ozone layer depletion could lead to the escalation of cancer-related diseases and the disruption of the ocean food chains.

The international arms trade, highly profitable for suppliers, is generating and sustaining conflicts in all parts of the world, with ever more sophisticated weapons increasing the scale of death and destruction. Illegal trade in arms is feeding terrorism that has emerged as the violent alternative to peaceful change between and within countries. International trade in narcotics and drugs, in spite of stringent border controls, appears to be growing all the time. And no border controls, however sophisticated, can stem the epidemic of Aids that is now threatening millions of lives throughout the world.

Serious problems on the world's agenda are multiplying and need effective action at global level. Yet the world's existing institutions are mostly much too weak and divided to face up to the issues. Some 170 independent and sovereign states belonging to the United Nations find it difficult to coordinate their actions or reconcile their differences so as to resolve problems common to them. What is missing is the willingness and capacity to subordinate individual interests to the common good. International institutions need to be endowed with supranational powers and sanctions, so that their decisions become enforceable international law.

It is in this area that Europe offers a unique example. The European Community has been founded on the principle that its laws not only take precedence over national laws but, when enacted, themselves become national laws enforceable by the judiciary in each member country. It is the agreement of members to cede elements of their national sovereignty to the

Community that has enabled it to enact common legislation and ensure its observance. While it may be a long time before the world community will be ready to emulate Europe's example, the European Community could do much to help advance it.

SECURITY

The European Community's latest step in providing an example of the pooling of national sovereignties is contained in the Maastricht Treaty's provisions for a common foreign and security policy. Its primary objectives are to safeguard the common values, fundamental interests and the independence of the Union.

Progress towards these common objectives follows the global confrontation between East and West which, after the Second World War, dominated international relations for some 45 years. Europe's defence arrangements during that period took an over-riding priority over trade and economic relations. But the search for common security stimulated ever closer cooperation in spheres other than defence and thus fuelled European integration.

The Second World War ended with Europe's economy totally dislocated and on the point of collapse. The dominant powers in Europe were the United States of America and the Soviet Union. The latter, as devastated economically as the rest of the continent, maintained its dominance by military occupation. In their alliance, aimed at defeating Nazi Germany, capitalist America and Britain on the one hand and Marxist Russia on the other had subordinated their differences, but the alliance did not long survive the end of the war.

Churchill, in his Fulton speech in 1946, spoke of the consequences of Europe's division into two politically incompatible camps and urged a policy of strength and unity in the West. The division became explicit with the Soviet rejection of the Marshall Plan and the forceful imposition of communist governments in all the countries which they occupied.

Fearing further Soviet expansion, Britain, France and the three Benelux countries signed a joint defence pact in March 1948 in Brussels. Following the Soviet blockade of Berlin, negotiations took place to establish a North Atlantic security system. In April 1949 the USA and Canada signed the North Atlantic Treaty with ten European countries: that is, the five Brussels

Treaty signatories and Denmark, Iceland, Italy, Norway and Portugal. Greece and Turkey joined in 1952, Germany in 1955 and Spain in 1982.

From then on, the world's two competing superpowers directly confronted each other in Europe, armed to the teeth and ready for instant war. To maintain their security both sides tried to sustain sufficient armed forces to deter each other. The mutual deterrence no doubt helped to provide some forty years of peace in Europe, though at considerable risk and cost. Purely military protection has always been unstable, for security gained through greater armed strength by one side makes the other insecure. Thus the arms race is sustained and ever more sophisticated strategies are developed to justify it. Each upward twist of the arms race increases the risk of accident or miscalculation.

Genuine security means much more than military balance. It requires the development of mutual trust between countries, treaties whose observance can be monitored, and machinery for the peaceful settlement of differences. Beyond that it should extend to cooperation in economic, social and political spheres, leading to a growing interdependence between nations which ensures permanent common security.

The goal of common security was, after all, the main motivating force behind the decision of the European countries, after the war, to unite to put centuries of internecine war behind them. The European Community, by developing common interests, policies, laws and institutions, has become the embodiment of such a system of common security. War between its member states is now inconceivable: indeed, it is no longer feasible.

The escalating cost of modern weaponry had put immense pressure on both superpowers to reduce their defence expenditure and commitments. The American contribution to the defence of Europe, through NATO, had until recently cost more than $150 billion a year. Economic and political pressures in America had led to reductions in their defence expenditure on Europe. The former Soviet Union's huge defence commitment, estimated to have devoured annually more than 15 per cent of GNP, had starved the domestic market of scarce resources and contributed to the dramatic changes introduced by Gorbachev when he came to power.

These pressures led the two superpowers to negotiate the INF Treaty, covering the removal of a whole class of intermediate nuclear weapons from Europe. Further major reductions of strategic nuclear weapons were subsequently achieved through the new START treaties which, by the end of the century, will reduce American and Russian nuclear arms to some 5,000 warheads each.

CSCE

The Conference on Security and Cooperation in Europe provides a new framework for safeguarding peace and security in our continent. Its origins go back to 1954, when Soviet Foreign Minister Vyacheslav Molotov proposed a European Security Conference to work out a collective security agreement. In the 1960s the idea was further developed within the Warsaw Pact under the so-called Rapacki Plan, launched by the Polish foreign minister. In 1969 the Warsaw Pact issued an 'Appeal to all European Countries' to assemble a general conference to consider questions of European security and peaceful cooperation. The initiative received cautious approval from the West, which insisted, however, on the inclusion of the USA and Canada. The Finnish government offered to host the conference, which first met in Helsinki in 1972. The CSCE was thus born with a membership that included all European states, except Albania, as well the two North American countries.

The Helsinki Final Act, adopted in 1975, included four so-called 'baskets' of diverse groups of subjects. These were: security dealing with inter-state relations and military issues; cooperation in economic relations, science, technology and the environment; cultural relations including freer movement of people, information and ideas; and progress towards the establishment of a permanent body for European security and cooperation. Subsequent negotiations took place at follow-up meetings held in Belgrade in 1977, Madrid in 1980–3 and in Vienna in 1989.

Then a summit conference was held in Paris in 1990, which issued the 'Charter of Paris for a New Europe'. Held in the aftermath of the collapse of the Soviet empire, the meeting welcomed the changed face of Europe and resolved to establish for it a system that would guarantee democracy, political pluralism, free elections and the rule of law. To these ends it set up a number of permanent institutions including a secretariat in Prague, an Office of Free Elections in Warsaw and a Conflict

Prevention Centre in Vienna. In 1992 the Warsaw Office of Free Elections was expanded into an Office for Democratic Institutions and Human Rights, and a Commissioner for Human Rights was appointed. The Charter of Paris marked a major turning point from CSCE's previous search for cooperation between two opposing political and economic systems to a forum of assistance to states making a transition to a new system of common values.

The Paris Summit was followed in 1992 with Council of Ministers' meetings held once or twice a year, culminating in a major review conference to be held in Budapest in 1994. Following the break-up of the Soviet Union, Yugoslavia and Czechoslovakia, the CSCE's membership increased to some 53 countries. All the participating states have an equal voice – there is no weighting or majority. Decisions are taken by consensus. None of the agreements concluded under the CSCE process are treaties and cannot therefore be legally binding on the participating states. However, at the Prague meeting in 1992 an important decision was taken on the safeguarding of human rights, democracy and the rule of law. It was agreed that action could be taken, involving political steps against a state judged guilty of clear, gross and uncorrected violation of CSCE commitments, without the consent of the guilty state. This introduced a new principle of 'consensus minus one'.

The new principle was first used in suspending Yugoslav participation in the CSCE process. The Yugoslav conflict has led to wide-ranging discussions and repeated political statements condemning the gross violation of human rights. Fact-finding missions were sent, and are stationed in Kosovo, Sandjak and Vojvodina as part of conflict-prevention measures. Beyond these, however, the CSCE has been unable to intervene in resolving interstate or internal conflicts except by goodwill missions and offers of mediation and conciliation.

A new Forum for Security Cooperation on military issues was also established in 1992 to start negotiations on arms control, disarmament and confidence and security building measures aimed at reducing risks of future conflicts. It is hoped that the negotiations will, in due course, establish a viable and permanent CSCE security order. The continuing principle of decisions by consensus makes it difficult to envisage that Europe's security against future conflicts can be left to the CSCE process alone.

NATO

In spite of progress towards a common security system in Europe, likely to emerge from the CSCE negotiating process, there is genuine reluctance within the North Atlantic Treaty Organisation (NATO) to see its own demise. Its members do not want to see the USA decouple itself from Europe, but recognise that the relative decline of American economic power must lead to the progressive reduction in its military preponderance within the alliance. To counteract this the European Community, or at any rate its members that belong to NATO, need to build a more cohesive European defence identity.

This means the creation of an effective European defence pillar with a number of developments. One prerequisite is common arms procurement, which would significantly reduce costs and at the same time make cooperation between armed forces of the European countries much more effective. If requirements are to be rationalised and economies in research and development achieved, there must be a single European defence budget for research and development and the joint arms requirements will have to be determined by a European arms procurement agency. This could be created out of the present Independent European Planning Group (IEPG) but with a Director General and a permanent Secretariat.

The second requirement is a much closer military integration of the forces of the European allies. NATO forces are already remarkably well-integrated, but what is still missing is the full integration of the French and Spanish forces within a common infrastructure and command system, and with common strategies. The French armed forces of 300,000 and its nuclear deterrent, plus some 200,000 Spanish troops, fully integrated into a common defence force, would greatly strengthen the European pillar of the Alliance.

Even though French opinion has in recent years moved towards closer participation in the Western Alliance, it is unlikely that France would be prepared to return to the NATO command structure. This explains developments which include the setting up of a Franco-German Defence Council and a common brigade. Helmut Schmidt in his Adolphe Bentinck Lecture in Paris in February 1987 proposed the replacement of NATO forces in Europe by a Franco-German army under a French general and a

French nuclear umbrella. British, Italian and Benelux forces could become associated. The Atlantic link would be maintained through the presence of two or three American divisions on the European continent. This proposal, however, is only piecemeal and begs many questions.

The key lies in developing a common philosophy on defence and its role within possible political developments beyond the NATO area. There is need for a common assessment of the perceived threats of future aggressions and the balance of forces needed, as well as a clear political objective for future action.

NATO's cohesive role over past decades has many attractions for the new democracies in Central and Eastern Europe. Following the dissolution of the Warsaw Pact and, in spite of CSCE arrangements, several of the new democracies feel exposed to potential threats to their security that could arise if democracy in the former Soviet republics failed and new authoritarian regimes emerged. Of particular concern to them would be potential threats from a nuclear-armed Russia, who might wish to reverse the dissolution of its former empire. For these reasons, some of Central and Eastern European countries have asked to be admitted into NATO and thus to come under the West's nuclear umbrella. NATO's response was not enthusiastic to the suggestion, which would extend its commitments beyond the frontiers of NATO's existing member states, but some form of association with them is being considered.

The real problem is that the North Atlantic Alliance was set up with a primary objective of defence against the Soviet Union and its satellites. For this purpose its defence role has now disappeared. Furthermore, NATO has hitherto strictly limited its activities to defending its member states and has been precluded by the treaty terms from intervention in conflicts out of its area of concern. That is why NATO as such has played no role in the Gulf and Yugoslav conflicts.

WESTERN EUROPEAN UNION

To fill the gap and enable the European Union to act in its own defence, the Maastricht Treaty has helped to revive a hitherto moribund European organisation. The Brussels joint defence pact concluded in 1948 set up the Western European Union (WEU), not much more than an intergovernmental discussion forum with a Council of Ministers and Parliamentary Assembly meeting at regular intervals, but with no real role once NATO was established.

For a number of years before Maastricht, attempts had been made to revitalise WEU as a way of strengthening the European pillar of the Atlantic Alliance, though all along there has been a difference of opinion about its purpose. Some of its members, principally the French, have seen WEU as the military arm of the emerging European Union. Britain wants WEU to act as a bridge between the European and American parts of the Atlantic Alliance. The Americans have been suspicious of any effective role for WEU that might provide Europe with greater independence from the USA and could become the embryo of a Western European military superpower with French and British nuclear weapons to back it. The emergence of yet another major military player could, in their view, threaten the existing peace order established by the Atlantic Alliance and encourage isolationist sentiments in America, which would welcome a significant reduction in its military commitments to the defence of Europe.

To bridge the differences, the Maastricht Treaty formally requested WEU to accept a new role as an integral part of the proposed European Union that would involve it in implementing decisions and actions of the Union with defence implications. Policies of the Union in this sphere would not, however, be allowed to prejudice treaty obligations of those members that belong to NATO. In a special declaration appended to the Maastricht Treaty, the members of WEU accepted the need to develop a genuine European security and defence identity leading to a common defence policy within the European Union and ultimately to a common defence, but one that would be compatible with that of the Atlantic Alliance. Thus WEU will become the defence component of the European Union as well as a means of strengthening the European pillar of the Atlantic Alliance.

The particular merit of WEU is that, unlike NATO, it is free to act outside the NATO area and could thus more easily intervene in conflicts such as Yugoslavia and beyond. The membership of WEU already includes nine out of the twelve Community members (the three Benelux countries, Britain, France, Germany, Italy, Portugal and Spain). In the declaration appended to the Maastricht Treaty, the remaining Community members were invited to become full members or observers. Other European states belonging to NATO, but not to the Community, have been invited to become associate members of WEU so that they can participate fully in its activities.

FOREIGN POLICY

Defence is an instrument of foreign policy and is thus incorporated in the Maastricht Treaty's provision for a Common Foreign and Security Policy. Its foreign policy elements are defined as the promotion of international cooperation, including the development and consolidation of democracy, the rule of law, and respect for human rights and fundamental freedoms. Its principal objective is to preserve peace and strengthen international security in accordance with the principles of the United Nations Charter and of the CSCE Paris Charter.

The Community's own experience in building cooperation and promoting peace among its members provides a useful model for others. Interdependence generated by integration has made war between its members not only unthinkable but no longer practicable. Europe's living standards, as the world's largest trader, largely depend on the preservation of peace in the rest of the world. Thus, any measures which reduce the risks of war must be of primary concern. Conservation of the world's natural resources is equally important for the world's biggest importer of food and raw materials. Growth in its own prosperity depends on the living standards and purchasing power of its trading partners also rising. That is why the European Community, more than most, has a direct interest in helping developing countries to grow out of their poverty. That is also why the European Community needs a single foreign policy that actively pursues its common interests.

How, then, can Europe play a world role that is commensurate with its potential? In wealth, expressed in its total gross domestic product, the Community is now second to none. Coupled with its share of world trade it is an economic giant, but politically it is still a pygmy. The reason is that, except for issues of trade and external commercial relations, foreign policy hitherto has not formed part of the Community's own responsibilities. All that has happened up to now is that, in certain limited fields, foreign policies of individual member states were being coordinated. The original Rome Treaties made no mention of foreign policy. A degree of cooperation in foreign affairs was achieved only as a result of the Davignon Report of 1970, which recommended a system to 'harmonise points of view, concert attitudes and, where possible, lead to common decisions'.

Acceptance of the Davignon Report led to the development of so-called 'political cooperation'. For several years this involved quarterly meetings of foreign ministers, kept strictly separate from Community business, though more recently both types of business have tended to be transacted at the same meetings. In addition, Political Directors, appointed by each foreign minister, met every month with day-to-day communications assured by a special telex system.

The Single European Act codified the system by formally committing member states to 'endeavour jointly to formulate and implement a European foreign policy'. This was to be achieved by close consultation on any foreign policy matters of general interest, so that convergence of positions and joint action could follow. The European Commission and the European Parliament were to be fully associated with the proceedings of political cooperation. Finally, every effort was made to ensure that the external policies of the European Community concerned with economic affairs should be consistent with foreign affairs pursued under the system of European Political Cooperation. To help it, a secretariat, under the direction of a committee of the Political Directors of member countries, was set up in Brussels to prepare and implement the activities of European Political Cooperation.

The Maastricht Treaty has taken this further. The Council of Ministers is entrusted with defining common foreign policy positions on any matter of general interest and member states are obliged to conform to them. In international organisations and at conferences, member states will have to coordinate their actions and uphold common positions through their diplomats and representatives. The Council of Ministers will arrive at common positions and take action by unanimity, but may also define certain matters on which decisions could be taken by qualified majority vote. On all external affairs the country holding the six months' presidency of the Council will represent the Union, but the European Commission will be associated with the Presidency's tasks. The European Parliament will be consulted on the main aspects of the common foreign and security policy and kept informed about its development.

Under the Treaty the common policy will be conducted outside the normal Community's institutional framework and not be subject to the European Court of Justice. Because of the European Parliament's very limited consultative role there is a denial of full democratic accountability to it for the Council's actions, and this perpetuates the democratic deficit over issues of foreign policy and security of the Union. It is to be hoped that the next revision of the Treaty in 1996 will merge this area within the Community's institutional framework and thus secure democratic control over issues as vital as those of war and peace.

NORTH–SOUTH

Even before more competences for external affairs are transferred to the European Community's own institutions, as recommended above, much more can be done in the economic field where the Community and its institutions are already largely responsible. Apart from issues of peace or war, it is the North–South divide that presents the greatest threats and challenges to humanity today. The Community has a better record in this field than most other developed countries. In 1991 the Community and its member states provided more than Ecu 21 billion (£17 bn) in development assistance, which is more than 40 per cent of all aid made available globally. Much more needs to be done, however, to tackle underdevelopment in the Third World, with its damaging consequences for all of us.

Despite progress over the past twenty years, some 3,000 million people in the Third World live on an annual income that is less than the monthly income of people in industrialised societies. In many countries it is no more than one-fiftieth of that enjoyed on average in the European Community. The consequences for the poorest are malnutrition, illiteracy, unemployment, illness and epidemics. Some 400 million children already suffer from serious nutritional deficiency.

The principal causes of underdevelopment stem from high birth rates and the underemployment of the expanding population, as well as from limited or underexploited natural resources. Most Third-World countries are not able to satisfy their own basic needs, let alone export surpluses to enable them to buy the products they lack. Owing to population growth, the Third World's cereal imports grew from 25 million to 80 million tonnes between 1960 and 1980 and could grow to more than 200 million by the end of this century. Inadequate local food prices discourage production, while climatic disasters such as floods or droughts can destroy several years' work. Through indiscriminate exploitation of such resources as forests and inappropriate cultivation of cleared lands, the natural environment is being gradually destroyed in many parts of the world. Each year an area twice the size of Belgium turns to desert. At this rate, one-quarter of the earth's surface is in danger of becoming a desert within twenty-five years. The vast watershed of the Himalayas is being transformed as forests are felled to provide more agricultural land. The deforested area no longer absorbs the snows and monsoons, which lead to massive floods that have devastated Bangladesh. Tropical rain forests are being felled and burnt indiscriminately at a rate which, if continued, will result in the total disappearance of rain forests within 85 years. Some of them in West Africa, Malaysia, Indonesia and the Philippines are unlikely to survive much beyond the end of this century.

Many Third-World economies, operating under a system first established by and for their former colonial masters, have depended for their exports on just a few primary products needed by the richer world. Between the 1950s and the 1990s prices of many primary products fell by more than half in real terms. Such worsening of the terms of trade have led to a massive imbalance between imports and exports, a reduction of purchasing power and a growing deterioration of the financial position of poorer countries. To survive, they have gone into deep debt with high interest rates. The total debt of developing countries by 1988 was some $1300 billion, equivalent to not far off double their annual export earnings. On average, interest payments absorb nearly one-fifth of export earnings. For some heavily indebted countries interest payments absorb up to half of their export earnings.

To break out of this vicious downward spiral urgent action must be taken by the rest of the world community, and especially the rich countries of Europe, North America, Japan and Australasia. The priorities are: combating hunger and protecting the environment from further destruction; dealing with debt; stimulating trade, production and investment; and generally assisting regional development.

The European Community's own record to date has not been bad. Its policies for Third-World countries stemmed from the

agreement in the original Rome Treaty to provide for the association with the Community of the former colonial territories of
Belgium, France, Italy and the Netherlands. With British, Spanish
and Portuguese accession the number of former colonies so
associated increased, and now some eighty-one countries in Africa, the Carribbean and Pacific (known as the ACP countries)
are linked under the so-called Lomé conventions, which are
renegotiated every five years. These are administered by common
institutions on a basis of equality between the Community and its
Third World partners.

Under the conventions some 99.5 per cent of the goods ex-
ported to the Community by the ACP countries are free of
customs duties, with no reciprocal concessions required on their
part. Some exceptions relate to farm produce, which enjoys
protection under the CAP, and quantitative limitations on textiles under the Multifibre Arrangement. Development aid
includes both grants and low-interest loans and has risen to some
ECU 8.5 billion for the latest five-year period up to 1990. A
particular feature of aid has been the so-called Stabex fund,
which compensates countries heavily dependent on one or more
staple products for severe fluctuations in their export earnings.
A similar system, called Sysmin, applies to mineral products.

The aid is concentrated on rural and agricultural development, on projects assisting small and medium-sized enterprises,
and on feasibility studies for industrial projects and productive
infrastructure such as ports, railways, water supplies and telecommunications. The Lomé conventions are not, however, to be
regarded as charitable. The Community's self-interest, so dependent on the supply of basic commodities and raw materials from
the Third World, lies in the rapid development of poorer countries that will in due course provide valuable markets for
Community products.

While priority is given to the ACP countries, aid and trading
concessions are also granted to other Third-World countries. The
aid falls under two categories. The first provides food and emergency aid to countries suffering from natural catastrophes or
other crises. Then there are bilateral and regional agreements,
under which development aid is included, with such countries as
India, Pakistan, Bangladesh, Sri Lanka and, in Latin America, the
five members of the Andean Pact and the six countries of the
Central American isthmus. In all, some 107 Third-World countries

had concluded cooperation agreements with the Community by 1989, and development projects were under way in 92 countries.

Trade concessions are principally under a system of generalised preferences, which are granted to all developing countries without discrimination and are not reciprocal. They involve the total suspension of customs duties, subject however to quota limits or ceilings which are reviewed each year to take account of the growth of international trade. They apply to all finished or semi-finished industrial products and to some 400 processed agricultural products.

Cooperation agreements, which give duty-free access to most industrial products and specific concessions for agricultural produce, have been negotiated with some twelve Mediterranean countries (i.e. all except Albania and Libya), and with the six countries of the Association of South East Asian Nations (ASEAN).

All the Community's programmes of assistance to the Third World represent an impressive effort, accounting for more than 40 per cent of all world aid given, but they still fall far short of the UN target of devoting at least 0.7 per cent of GNP to aid. Of all the member countries only Denmark and the Netherlands have reached the target. Furthermore, the Community's agricultural policy has encouraged the dumping of food surpluses on world markets, at times in competition with Third-World farmers. Much more needs to be done if the agreed objectives of the Community's policies towards the Third World are to be realised.

The highest priority must clearly be given to action to eliminate the causes of hunger. China and India have been most successful in ending their recurrent famines. The problem is largely confined to Africa. What we need to do is to help individual farmers to improve their skills, encourage appropriate land reform, set up proper marketing systems, build roads, and increase prices to producers so that they will stay on the land. Under the Lomé Convention the Community should do a deal with the appropriate ACP countries, so that increased development aid will be directed towards agriculture in return for a coordinated programme designed to achieve the outlined objectives.

Both in the context of combating the causes of hunger and in helping development generally, high priority must be given to safeguarding the environment. In return for debt relief measures, developing countries would have to guarantee to maintain their stock of renewable resources and conserve those that cannot be renewed. Funds would only be released for projects which conform to laid-down environmental criteria. A multinational World Environment Trust should be set up, which, again in return for debt relief, would acquire and preserve rainforests and generally control the exploitation of environmentally sensitive commodities.

The Maastricht Treaty sets out the objectives of the Community's development policy. These are: sustainable economic and social development of developing countries with special help being channelled to the least advanced countries; a gradual and smooth integration of the developing countries with the world economy; and the campaign against poverty.

In addition to aid, debt relief and investment, the principal contribution that the Community can make to help developing countries out of bankruptcy and build up their economies is through increased trade. This involves a further opening up of the Community's own markets, helping to promote trade between developing countries among themselves, and playing a positive role within the United Nations Conference on Trade and Development (UNCTAD) to improve the functioning of the international system. To increase purchasing power and employment of Third-World countries, European industry should be encouraged to enter into production-sharing arrangements with local enterprises, and a European Community Export Credit Agency should be established, with uniform credit rates for imports from the Community. In all these trading transactions the ECU should be used, as it would provide a more stable currency for trade with the Community and among developing countries themselves.

Finally, the Community should take the initiative in developing its relations with potential regional leaders and the regions they represent, such as Brazil, Mexico, India, China, Egypt, Nigeria and the ASEAN countries. The objective should be to encourage the co-management of the world's most urgent problems and to assist them to grow into viable economic regions. More united, the regions would be better able to tackle common problems of environmental breakdown, indebtedness and trade through the development of payments unions, trade financing agencies and common institutions to handle relations within regions. The Community itself should help in major regional environmental actions such as, for example, preventing repeated and disastrous floods in the Brahmaputra basin. In all these actions the European Community can play a crucial role in leading the world out of poverty and its present divisions, towards a greater unity of purpose.

RELATIONS BETWEEN RICH COUNTRIES

In its relationship with the richer northern world the European Community has an equally important role to play to bring stability and economic growth. During the first three decades after the Second World War, the world's economy developed in a way unequalled before or since. It grew within an international framework consciously established to promote growth. The General Agreement on Tariffs and Trade (GATT) was designed to free trade, and the Bretton Woods System and the International Monetary Fund (IMF) were set up to secure exchange rate stability and adequate resources to overcome balance of payments problems. The European Community itself showed the massive benefits of economic integration. Trade between its members grew twelvefold in twenty-five years, while world trade grew fivefold.

The major hurdle encountered was the stalemate in the Uruguay Round of GATT, which is designed to extend free trade to services and reduce protection, especially in trade in agricultural products. The long-drawn-out battle between the USA and the Community over agricultural subsidies was at the root of the delays, but many other restrictions to free trade still need to be resolved.

The devaluation of the US dollar in 1972, the development of floating exchange rates, and the quadrupling of oil prices and those of most raw materials following the 1973 Israel–Arab war, slowed growth and introduced new barriers to trade through wild currency fluctuations, fuelled by speculation and vast, volatile flows of capital. Trade and investment suffered, while high rates of inflation forced deflationary policies. With the breakdown of monetary stability, protectionism reared its ugly head again, while excessively high exchange rates eliminated competitive industries in some countries. One result has been mass unemployment at levels not seen since the 1930s. Another was growing parsimony in aid towards the Third World. US aid, for instance, tumbled from 2.4 per cent of its GNP in 1948 to 0.2 per cent during the Reagan administration, and much of what remained was in the form of military assistance, whereas US contributions to world agencies had been cut drastically.

What can Europe do to reverse the trend and bring back some greater order to international economic relations? Already, by having a single identity in trade and commercial relations with the world outside, the European Community has succeeded in changing the balance of power and contributing towards the establishment of a more orderly world system. The Dillon, Kennedy and Tokyo rounds of tariff reductions, and the success with which the worst features of protectionism have been kept at bay during the past decade, have been due largely to the Community's single voice in trade matters and the influence it brought to bear as an equal partner of the Americans. In contrast the lack of a common European role in monetary or macro-economic policies, quite apart from foreign and defence policies, has meant that its influence has been much less effective on the international scene.

It is in this context that the Community's Maastricht commitment to Economic and Monetary Union and a Common Foreign and Security Policy is so important. Once both are implemented Europe will gain an equal voice with Japan and America. Once the ECU replaces most Community currencies, three world currencies will emerge that could lead towards global exchange rate stability. By promoting greater harmony between their respective macro-economic policies, the countries managing the three world currencies would be able to reduce the uncontrolled movement of capital in the international financial markets. Closer cooperation could lead to the strengthening of the IMF and the World Bank, including the development of new assets to fuel and sustain the growth of world trade. Finally, an economically united Europe would have more self-confidence to promote freer world trade and combat protectionist tendencies at home and among their main trading partners.

POLITICAL UNION

The case for the European Community to act as one in defence of its interests throughout the world is obvious. That is why the extension of its competences to all aspects of foreign policy, including defence, is so important. A European Political Union with a common foreign and defence policy would transform the world scene fundamentally. Some might fear the emergence of another superpower, but as the world's largest trading unit, which is also strategically vulnerable, Europe must be capable of defending and furthering its interests. These include a further reduction of trading barriers. The European Union should also want to see the developing countries grow economically and thus offer new markets for Europe's exporters. Monetary and economic stability would provide the framework within which a new world economic order could emerge.

European initiatives to encourage regional unity in Latin America, Africa and Asia, on lines similar to those pursued within Europe, could help other continents to reduce local conflicts and promote regional cooperation. Growing economic interdependence within regions and between them would lay the foundations for a world free from local or general wars. Common global problems such as the protection of the environment and conservation of the world's scarce resources would be easier to pursue. It would also be easier to curtail indiscriminate trade in arms, promote international action to combat the drugs trade, and organise effective measures to defeat terrorism. The habit of cooperation would demonstrate that a world order guaranteeing peace and growing prosperity is within reach. From there, the next step could be to provide the whole of our planet with a system of enforceable international law under the authority of a world government with strictly limited but real powers.

UNITED NATIONS

After the end of the East–West confrontation, progress towards such a world government is no longer beyond imagination. The United Nations (UN) organisation has greatly enhanced its authority by the willingness of all the permanent Security Council members to support its efforts to resolve international crises. The veto powers, possessed by the USA, Russia, China, France and Britain have not been used, and there has been a growing trend to entrust the UN with ever more ambitious peace-keeping missions. Just to mention a few more recent ones, they have ranged from Cambodia in Asia, Lebanon in the Middle East, Somalia in

Africa and Yugoslavia in Europe. Furthermore, the UN's humanitarian aid is constantly growing.

Conflict prevention measures are, however, not enough. Peace enforcement, on lines developed following the Gulf War, is under increasing discussion, as is the reform of the United Nations to make it able to take prompt and decisive action. Britain and France, as Europe's two permanent members of the Security Council, could take the initiative. More countries of major weight in world affairs should become permanent members of the Security Council. Japan, Germany and India are among the obvious candidates. But such an enlargement of permanent members should be accompanied by the removal of their veto powers.

Such a radical proposal may not yet be practical politics, but the European countries could give a lead. If Britain, France and Germany were permanent members of the Security Council, they should renounce their individual rights to veto decisions, reserving this power to cases where all three countries exercised it together. This would provide a first step for the European Union to act as one within the Security Council, but also offer hope, by its example, that one day the world community might operate without individual countries, however important, having any veto powers.

Finally, world security demands an end to the possible use of nuclear weapons, which still pose a potential threat to the very survival of the human race. This has become ever more urgent, following Iraq's attempts to become a nuclear power and the dissolution of the Soviet Union and its centralised control over its own nuclear weapons. An increasing number of states are technologically capable of building such weapons and others might be able to purchase the technology. The manufacture and possession of nuclear weapons, cannot be abolished without effective sanctions.

The solution may lie in the establishment of a World Security Authority, at whose disposal the principal nuclear powers should be persuaded to place their nuclear capabilities, and to which Britain and France should be among the first to pledge their support. The powers of the Authority, under UN control, would initially be confined to deterring any country from using or threatening to use such weapons. In time, the Authority could develop into the military arm of the United Nations, with the right to call on member states to provide armed forces for the implementation of UN policies in preserving peace and security throughout the world.

Chapter 9

The future

History is shaped not so much by events as by circumstances leading up to them and by reactions to them afterwards. This definition helps to explain the reasons for the movement towards European integration and the way in which it has progressed, and it can assist in charting the probable course of events to come. The reaction to the carnage of the First World War was an attempt to regulate international relations by voluntary agreement between fully sovereign nation states within the League of Nations. The ideas floated then about creating a European federation to prevent war and promote cooperation were not accepted or even understood. The League failed in its objectives because it lacked authority and sanctions to enforce its decisions. The lessons of its failure – which led to the Second World War – were, however, learnt; and former enemies in Europe decided to create supranational institutions whose decisions would become legally binding upon the participating states.

The European Coal and Steel Community, set up in 1951, implemented the principle of supranationality by establishing a High Authority that was independent of governments. While its institutional system was of a pre-federal nature, in his declaration which led to the establishment of the ECSC, Robert Schuman saw it 'as a first step in the federation of Europe' although he recognised that 'Europe will not be made at once or according to a single overall plan'. Against the background of the cold war in Europe and actual military conflict in Korea the next obvious step in European integration seemed to be in the field of defence and political unification. It led to the signing of the European Defence Community Treaty in 1952 and negotiations for the establishment of a European Political Community in parallel.

However, the lessening of international tension, following the death of Stalin in 1953, removed the urgency for defence integration and, following the failure of the French Parliament to ratify the EDC Treaty, progress towards political and defence unity was arrested.

The impetus towards unity was maintained, however, by building on the success of European economic cooperation, stimulated by the Marshall Plan which led to the establishment of the Organisation for European Economic Cooperation and the European Payments Union. Successful negotiations that followed the collapse of the EDC Treaty resulted in the treaties setting up the European Economic Community and Euratom. This time, the treaties were ratified and came into force in 1958. The timetable for setting up the common market under the EEC Treaty was not only kept, but actually implemented ahead of its target date.

In the meantime, however, the collapse of the Fourth French Republic, which brought General de Gaulle to power in 1958, had a profound though temporary effect on the development of the European Community. France was its leading member and de Gaulle was opposed to supranationality. As long as he remained in power further progress towards European unity was delayed. Once he resigned in 1969 the process was restarted. The Community was enlarged from six to nine members. It acquired its own financial resources and resolved to achieve a European Union by 1980.

Progress towards this was marked by commitment to move towards Economic and Monetary Union and to the development of political cooperation. But the world oil crisis in 1973 and the massive rise in prices of most primary products stimulated a rapid rise in inflation and major monetary instability. Efforts to construct the Economic and Monetary Union collapsed and progress to full Union was delayed. Agreement was reached, however, to elect the European Parliament by direct universal suffrage and to make another attempt at monetary unification through the establishment of the European Monetary System in 1979.

The process towards political unification followed. Yet another solemn declaration to transform all relations between member states into a European Union was signed in Stuttgart in 1983 by ten Heads of Governments (Greece having joined in the meantime). The European Parliament produced its own Draft Treaty for European Union in 1984. Negotiations for a single internal market that followed were partly influenced by the Parliament's Draft Treaty, but also by a growing awareness that continuing non-tariff barriers between member countries were making the Community increasingly uncompetitive in trading relations with the USA and Japan.

The resulting Single European Act, which came into force in 1987, aimed not only at the effective removal of internal Community frontiers by 1992, but also committed the signatories to a full Economic, Monetary and Political Union of Europe. This commitment led to the Maastricht Treaty which laid down the steps towards Economic and Monetary Union before the end of the century and laid the foundations for a Political Union. Further treaty reforms are envisaged in 1996. In the meantime negotiations are taking place for the further enlargement of the European Community of the Twelve to perhaps sixteen members by 1996 and the prospect of several subsequent enlargements. During the next twenty years this could lead to a European Union of between twenty and thirty member states. If a union, double the present size, is to survive as a cohesive group it will need further institutional reforms on federal lines. These will have to define, even more clearly than hitherto, the powers of the European institutions that are clearly necessary for running an effective union and the powers reserved to national, regional and local levels of government to accommodate the wide diversity of the peoples belonging to the Union.

The story so far illustrates that progress towards some form of European federation, commenced in 1950, has proceeded ever since, even if by stops and starts. The stage of integration already reached, over a relatively short period when measured against other major developments in world history, has been quite remarkable. Each major step forward in the process hitherto has, after all, depended on unanimous agreement between participating states, none of whom was forced to agree.

PUBLIC OPINION

Are individual citizens ready to accept these objectives and the changes needed to achieve them? Very substantial and comprehensive data are available on public attitudes on Europe. Ever since 1973 the European Commission's Directorate of Information has been commissioning independent research institutes to conduct extensive public opinion surveys twice a year. All the institutes employed belong to the European Society for Opinion and Market Research, which lays down strict standards for their members. The surveys conducted in Britain are by Gallup Poll. The sample for each survey is about 12,000 interviewees carefully divided by the size of populations living in 138 regions within the Community of twelve countries. To secure results that would ensure less than a 5 per cent margin of error, not less than 1,000 interviews are conducted in each member country, with the exception of Luxembourg where the figure is 300. Fifteen years of polling have confirmed their accuracy by the relative closeness of responses to identical questions in consecutive surveys, illustrating both the consistency and trend of opinions.

The so-called Eurobarometer of opinion provides extensive data on a wide range of issues of interest and has shown that generally opinions throughout the Community are fairly similar between its different member countries. Larger variations which show up often relate to the length of a country's membership of the Community. The six original members often appear more enthusiastic about Europe than some of the latecomers such as Denmark and the United Kingdom, though not Ireland, Spain or Portugal whose opinions are closer to those of the Six.

Each survey includes questions on the future development of the Community and the data quoted below are confined to those issues. A major survey on the future of Europe was published in March 1987 on the 30th anniversary of the signature of the Treaty of Rome, and the following responses were recorded on questions of direct relevance to our analysis of public attitudes:

Question: Are you personally for or against the European Community developing towards becoming a United States of Europe?

Of those who replied, 76 per cent were in favour throughout the Community. The figure for the original Six EC members was 83 per cent. The United Kingdom figure was 58 per cent. Denmark alone had a majority of 60 per cent against.

Question: After what time would you entrust the government of Europe with the responsibility for the economy, foreign affairs and defence?

The responses of those who chose the timescale of 'in the next twenty years' were 65 per cent throughout the Community. In the UK the figure was 58 per cent of those who replied.

Question: In the case of an election for the head of government of Europe, is it possible that you would vote for a candidate who was not of your nationality or would you rule it out?

Excluding those who expressed a conditional opinion, 69 per cent throughout the Community said yes as against 31 per cent who would rule it out. The comparative figures for the UK (which were the lowest among the twelve) show 54 per cent saying yes with 46 per cent opposed.

On the more complex question of national against a European identity, the survey sought attitudes on a graduated scale between the following two opinions on which interviewees were asked to indicate to which opinion they found themselves nearer:

Some say (A): If one day the countries of Europe were really united, this would mark the end of our national historic, cultural identity and our own national economic interests would be sacrificed.

Others say (B): The only way of protecting our national historic, cultural identities and our national economic interests against a challenge put up by the Great World Powers is for the countries of Europe to become truly united.

Of those who indicated an orientation towards one or the other of the above statements, excluding those who chose a middle position, the results showed 72 per cent throughout the Community favouring proposition (B) and 28 per cent favouring (A). The corresponding figures for the UK were 54 per cent for (B) and 46 per cent for (A). The only country showing a clearly adverse attitude to European unity was Denmark.

After the signature of the Maastricht Treaty the Eurobarometer carried out in the Spring of 1992 gave an illuminating account of public attitudes to the various subjects contained in the Treaty. The general judgment among those who had actually heard about the Treaty at the time showed that within the Community as a whole 86 per cent approved it. In Britain those in favour represented 78 per cent. All the respondents were also asked the following question on the allocation of responsibilities between the Community and national governments:

Question: Some people believe that certain areas of policy should be decided by national government while other areas should be decided jointly within the European Community.

Table 9.1

Policies Responsibilities to:	Total EC sample		UK alone	
	EC %	national %	EC %	national %
Foreign policy	77	23	70	30
Security and defence	59	41	46	54
Immigration	62	38	39	61
Economic and Monetary Union with an independent Central Bank	68	32	46	54
A single currency	60	40	37	63
Cooperation with developing countries	85	15	84	16
Protection of the environment	75	25	72	28
Research and development	80	20	77	23
Health and welfare	42	58	30	70
Education	42	58	26	74

The response of those who expressed a preference either for the EC or the national government for the different topics are given in Table 9.1 in percentages for the whole sample and also for the UK alone.

In the same survey the number of respondents in favour of granting the European Parliament full legislative powers to be exercised jointly with the Council of Ministers were 78 per cent for the whole Community, with 65 per cent in favour in the UK alone.

What these responses show, as do answers to many more questions that appear regularly in the twice-yearly Eurobarometer, is that a substantial majority of Community citizens are ready to see progress towards European union. As for the UK, public opinion, reflecting the more lukewarm attitude traditionally expressed by British governments, still appears to be in advance of many of their political leaders.

HAVING A SAY

Public opinion during the Maastricht ratification debates, which followed the above survey, fluctuated quite widely. After the narrow Danish rejection of the Treaty in its first referendum in June 1992, the Irish approved the treaty by nearly 70 per cent in theirs. When the French referendum campaign started early in the Summer, those in favour of ratification were more than two to one. Yet, by the end of the campaign the lead narrowed dramatically, with the Treaty approved by a mere 2 per cent majority. The public was not directly consulted in the other Community countries, but ratification received approval by overwhelming majorities within their respective parliaments. Opinion polls in those countries did, however, show that several of the issues raised by Maastricht were subjects of public disquiet and there was general criticism over inadequate information about the Treaty and its impact on people's everyday lives.

The problem is largely due to the complexity of the issues and the difficulty in explaining them adequately to obtain an informed public response. The author of this book was the national organiser of the referendum campaign in favour of British membership of the Community in 1975. The issues then were rather simpler and concerned a straightforward choice of Britain to be or not to be a member of the Community. British public opinion, tested when the decision to hold the referendum was first taken in 1974, showed a two-thirds majority against British membership. It took an intensive six-months' campaign for the issues to be widely debated and understood, before the public reversed its earlier opinion and approved membership by two to one.

Arguments in favour or against referenda have been rehearsed many times. Those against claim that in a parliamentary democracy decisions are the responsibility of the people's elected representatives. The principal argument in favour of referenda is that on major constitutional issues, which fundamentally change the way people are governed, the people should have a direct say. It is a matter of dispute whether the Maastricht Treaty does raise such fundamental constitutional issues. Progress to Maastricht has been incremental and it can be argued that the Single European Act, with qualified majority voting replacing unanimity on most legislative issues concerned with the Act, provided the real substantive shift from intergovernmental to supranational Community decisions and that Maastricht merely extended these to a number of other policy areas.

Nevertheless, if the European Union is to develop into a genuine federal United States of Europe, the case for citizens to give their direct consent for its formation becomes much more difficult to contest. Yet the problem remains about the complexity of the issues and the way these can be made comprehensible for an informed decision. Furthermore, the European Community up to now has largely dealt with issues that, in most instances, affect individual citizens only indirectly. Maastricht, for the first time, establishes the principle of a European citizenship, implying individual rights and duties. These are still fairly limited but, as recommended in Chapter 5, they are likely to be further extended. There is thus a growing need to make the ordinary citizens much more aware of the emerging Union and to help them to identify with it.

This could best be achieved by drafting a comprehensive constitution for the proposed federation. On this issue the Eurobarometer, conducted in 1988, asked whether the European Parliament should be entrusted with drafting such a constitution. Of those who expressed an opinion, 79 per cent throughout the Community favoured it. In the UK the figure in favour was 61 per cent. Considering the effect on national governments, the drafting of such a constitution should be the task of a special constitutional convention set up jointly by the European Parliament and national parliaments. The draft constitution emerging from the convention should be submitted for examination first to all the parliaments involved. In the light of the debates, a duly amended draft should then go to the European Council for approval. Once approved, the constitution should then be opened to a full public debate throughout the Union, with a final decision on its acceptance taken by a referendum of all the Union's citizens.

In this way, the legitimacy of the proposed federation would be fully established by the general will of the people. Participation in its adoption would furthermore ensure a much closer identification of the public with it and a popular acceptance of the rights and duties enshrined in the constitution. Experience in the USA demonstrates that, in spite of the wide diversity of backgrounds and cultures of its people, the constitution which guarantees their democratic rights is the bond which provides the citizens with their strong sense of belonging to the Union.

This bonding is even more relevant in the Union of European States, which will contain peoples speaking several different languages, of distinct cultures and identities and with a wide variety of ethnic groups and minorities. This is particularly important in the light of the disturbing growth of nationalist sentiments and the conflicts between ethnic minorities in the eastern part of our continent. A new approach to the concept of unity with diversity is needed. It requires a recognition that, within the Union, all of us belong to minorities. Even the most numerous – the German nation, numbering some 80 million – represents less than a quarter of the present Community's population and will fall further as a proportion of the future enlarged Union.

Ota Adler, a founder member of Federal Union in Britain before the Second World War, expressed this rather well in a speech in Antwerp in 1993. According to him 'a Union organised on federal lines, based on the principle of subsidiarity, will comprise large and small states and countries, making all of them – in effect – minorities, and within them other minorities, whether ethnic, religious or other groups with common bonds. All will be protected under a European constitution guaranteeing human rights to enjoy their distinct cultures, speak their own languages, follow their traditions and customs and preserve their individuality, subject only to the same rights extended to all'.

WHAT SORT OF FEDERATION?

The question then arises about what is actually involved in creating a federal United States of Europe. Since its inception in 1950, progress towards this objective is clearly well beyond the halfway stage. The Community has supranational institutions, including an embryo government in the form of the executive Commission, a fully empowered legislature in the Council of Ministers, a body of laws that is applicable throughout the Community and a Court of Justice whose rulings on constitutional issues and on individual laws are final and binding. The directly elected Parliament, while having to be consulted on all Community issues, still lacks full legislative powers, which it should possess in a parliamentary democracy.

What then are the changes and reforms necessary to transform the present Community into a full federation? As the Community's history shows, it will not happen overnight or by a single major reform. The process is continuous and usually emerges as a reaction to, and consequence of, previous changes and advances. The significance of the present stage of the Community's evolution lies in the Single European Act and the Maastricht Treaty, with consequences of their implementation.

These have transformed the economic Community of twelve member countries into a single economic unit, which heads of governments have recognised by their commitment to Economic and Monetary Union.

Progress to Economic and Monetary Union, as set out in the Maastricht Treaty, may undergo some changes due to the currency fluctuations that occurred within the Exchange Rate Mechanism in 1992–3. Greater economic convergence will be needed to re-establish stability. The system of mutual financial support for currencies will require further strengthening. For some countries, it may even lead to an earlier locking of their currencies than originally envisaged in the Treaty. This could involve the pooling of responsibilities and resources of the respective national central banks in support of the fixed system. Countries temporarily outside the ERM will be helped to come in again and the EMU, as set out in the Treaty, is likely to be established finally before the end of this century.

The effective completion of the internal market by the end of 1992 depended not merely on the removal of all barriers to trade including, in particular, the enforcement of common public procurement, but also on a coordinated and adequately financed European research and development programme for all advanced technology. To match the industrial and technological potential of its principal technologically advanced competitors in the non-military field, the Community should try to pattern its coordinating role on that of the Japanese Ministry of International Trade and Industry. In the field of defence, it should develop common arms procurement as well as a space programme, which, as in America, would stimulate technological innovation that would bring benefits throughout industry.

Paying for the suggested European research and development programme and common arms procurement needs financial resources that are not available to the Community under its existing budgetary arrangements. The decisions taken in Edinburgh in December 1992, on the financing of the Community until the end of the century, have provided increased financing for some of the policies in favour of greater cohesion, but they still remain very limited in scope.

This is not a plea for more public spending. On the contrary, twelve separate national expenditure budgets on research and development, and arms procurement, are bound to be much more costly and wasteful than financing single and coordinated policies in these areas. That is why an enlarged Community budget, replacing much of the duplicated national expenditures, would actually bring about major savings in public finance. Furthermore, a progressive system of Community taxation, related to the wealth of member states and their citizens, once spent on these programmes would have a significant redistributive effect and reduce the gap between the richer and poorer regions and sectors.

A budget of between 5 and 7 per cent of the Community's gross domestic product, according to the MacDougall Report, referred to in chapter 4, could have such a significant redistributive effect. Much more effective democratic control than at present of public expenditure at Community level would have to accompany any increase in its revenues. If the European Parliament and the Council of Ministers were actually responsible for raising taxes for the Community, which would directly impinge upon the taxpayers instead of coming out of national budgets, they would act more responsibly in controlling its expenditure.

The profound changes that have taken place as a result of the collapse of the communist system within the former Soviet block have opened up entirely new perspectives for the future of the Union. First, there is the changed security situation, which requires a new approach to safeguarding peace in Europe. The CSCE process, coupled with a new role for Western European Union, has lessened the need to rely on the defence aspects of the NATO alliance. Yet there will be a continued wish to retain American involvement in European security, which may have to be accommodated within a new, more political role for the Atlantic alliance. Then, there are now real prospects for a substantial enlargement of the Community, with several countries queuing up to join; this within the next ten years, could double the Community's present membership.

With a common foreign and security policy, Europe will be able to make a much more significant contribution to world affairs. Its interests as the world's largest trader depend on global peace and genuine economic growth, particularly in the developing world. Europe's interest in the latter is already shown by its 40 per cent share of all aid advanced to the Third World. The faster the Third World grows the bigger its markets for Community products and services. That is why Europe has a direct interest in finding solutions to the debt burden that inhibits further growth and development. Some solutions might well combine help to the debtors in return for their action to safeguard natural resources such as forests, the depletion of which is threatening our global climate and environment.

Europe has an even more significant role to play in changing international relationships and laying the foundations for a new world order with common governance. The experience of the European Community's own origins and progress towards a federation offers an example to other regions in the world that, like Europe, have suffered from conflicts and divisions. The Community has a unique vocation, based on its own experience, to promote regional unity in other parts of the world. Cooperation between integrating regional groups of countries could lead to the emergence of a world authority – with the capacity and power to promote balanced economic growth, conservation of the global environment and world peace – that would banish for ever the threat of a nuclear holocaust or, indeed, of any armed conflicts between countries.

BUILDING A FEDERATION

All these desirable and even noble objectives depend, however, on a Europe that is sufficiently united to be able to pursue them. That is why the Community must move towards becoming an effective federation that will have the capacity and authority to match the federal USA and other major powers. Of course, the European federation will not be patterned on those of other models. Its development has different historical origins and its own distinct institutional system. The federal system that is emerging in Europe is likely to be much less centralised than that of many other federations. It is being formed by consent by independent and sovereign nation states that have agreed to pool and share their sovereignty in clearly defined spheres of activity. Federal devolution within most member states is gaining momentum in parallel.

The federal method can offer solutions to otherwise intractable internal conflicts, such as, for instance, the language quarrels in Belgium, which are now being resolved by the setting up of three autonomous regions under a federal constitution. Spain provides another example of the use of federal responses to the democratic demands for regional autonomy after the throttling centralism of the Franco fascist era. Effective self-government and autonomy for Gibraltar within Spain might ultimately be acceptable to the inhabitants of Gibraltar provided that, as full citizens of a federal Europe, they would have their rights and autonomy guaranteed under the European constitution.

Might not a federal approach to the problems of Northern Ireland also offer some possible way out of the current impasse? Is it really beyond the wit of politicians to work out a system of autonomy and self-government for a province that would form part of an Irish federation while retaining a constitutional link with Britain? Is not such an approach likely, furthermore, to be more credible once both Ireland and Britain are full and equal member states within a European federation?

Such a European federation with the functions and powers outlined above would require some reform of existing Community institutions. The first and foremost objective must be to correct the democratic deficit that has been highlighted by the Single European Act and the Maastricht Treaty. Collective decisions of the Council of Ministers, especially when reached by majority, cannot be held accountable by twelve separate national parliaments. The European Parliament must acquire powers of co-decision with the Council in all spheres, including those reserved for intergovernmental decisions under Maastricht, in order to give the Union's legislation democratic legitimacy.

The choice of European Commissioners, who in effect form the cabinet of an embryo European government, should not consist of nominees chosen, often for idiosyncratic reasons, by national governments alone. Choice of Commissioners should be left to the President of the Commission in consultation with governments, and become subject to approval by the European Parliament. At present the President of the Commission is chosen by the heads of governments for a two-year term. Moving towards the direct election of the President by universal suffrage, for a term that starts at the same time as that of the European Parliament, would have a number of advantages. It would considerably enhance public interest in European affairs and secure much higher participation in the European parliamentary elections.

But the single most significant step in helping people to identify with Europe would be to draw up a constitution with clearly defined democratic rights and duties for its citizens, adopted by them directly in a referendum. The United States of Europe will never become a full reality until all its inhabitants feel themselves to be its citizens with a sense of belonging and a sense of loyalty towards it that is no weaker than that which they feel towards their nation, region and local community.

Shaping the future

If the case for the United States of Europe is a persuasive one, how is it actually to be brought about? On the face of it, decisions to transform the European Community into a full union lie first in the hands of national governments and then in those of national parliaments, which have to ratify any major reforms proposed by their governments. Parliaments in our democratic societies have to take account of public opinion, which develops in response to many influences, with the media playing a powerful role and opinion formers including spokesmen of major interests, such as commerce, industry and the trade unions, and individual politicians forming parliaments and governments. So the case for the United States of Europe needs first to be made to governments and their parliaments against a background of a favourable trend of public opinion.

An examination of the history of the evolution of the European Community illustrates the process. First and foremost came the ideas. The objective of a European federation was already promoted in the 1920s by the Pan-Europe Union founded by the Austrian Count Coudenhove-Kalergi. His ideas and those of the founders of Federal Union were developed by the Federal Union Research Institute set up under the chairmanship of Sir William Beveridge in Oxford in 1939. Many distinguished academics and political thinkers contributed to the development of a wide-ranging body of literature on the theory of federalism and its application to post-war Europe. Others, not directly involved in Federal Union, shared their objectives and promoted them in their own way. Of those Jean Monnet was, without doubt, the foremost example.

The ideas and more detailed proposals for action were then

communicated to political leaders who, once persuaded, were in a position to act. The first example of this was the proposal made in 1940 by Winston Churchill, backed by his cabinet, to create a Franco-British Union. The key to this process of persuasion of politicians lies in a formula expressed by Monnet: 'Although much time is required to attain power, only a small amount is required to explain to those who have it the way to solve actual difficulties... when ideas are lacking, they accept yours with gratitude, on condition that you allow them to claim paternity. Because they run the risks, they have need of laurels.'

The political leaders of Continental countries in exile in London and many in the resistance movements on the Continent during the war were much influenced and persuaded by the ideas of Federal Union and its publications. Many of them retained their commitment to a federal Europe after the war when they exercised positions of responsibility in their countries or in European forums. People such as like Paul Henri Spaak and Altiero Spinelli provide notable examples.

The ideas are of course communicated much more widely to opinion formers in all sectors of society, who then spread the message among their peers and through them to their followers and public. Particularly important in this context are those who are behind the decision-makers, including civil servants and close political friends and supporters. The other key group consists of the journalists who can communicate the message to the wider public. The process of communication takes a variety of forms. Apart from the written word in books, pamphlets and the media, conferences, seminars and lectures provide the opportunity for verbal communication. Thus verbal communication need not be confined to the issues to be promoted, but may well be introduced incidentally on platforms set up for discussion of other, though related topics. Then there are visible public demonstrations of support for the ideas which, by attracting media coverage, will in turn influence the politicians, who are always sensitive to public pressure.

Many of the ideas advanced in this book are those developed in much greater detail by experts in their respective subjects, who have undertaken research and participated in study groups and commissions set up to produce proposals for further progress in European integration. Foremost among these have been the study groups of the London-based Federal Trust for Research and

Education, which is the successor to William Beveridge's Federal Union Research Institute, and the Trans-European Policy Studies Association, set up by the Federal Trust and comprising authoritative research institutes in other European Community countries. Other proposals stem from the reports of commissions formed on the initiative of the European Community institutions and from books on the subjects covered.

Several of the proposals, summarised here, have been disseminated widely and have already played a significant role in influencing opinion formers, including politicians and their leaders throughout the Community. The process of continuous public education on European issues has over the years fallen to voluntary organisations, such as the European Movement, operating in some thirty European countries, and its individual membership organisation the Union of European Federalists. Their role has been extensive and influential ever since their first combined Congress of Europe in the Hague in 1948, held under the chairmanship of Winston Churchill.

The European Movement, which is primarily an umbrella organisation for all types of organisations with an interest in European affairs, keeps in touch with associations of individuals in every sector of society. This includes political parties, industry, commerce, trade unions, employers associations, most professions, educational establishments and special-interest organisations. The methods of disseminating ideas vary widely, from the organisation of conferences and distribution of publications to the supply of speakers to address audiences of every variety from platforms provided by other organisations.

The Union of European Federalists consists of individual members within the European Movement and provides a valuable forum for its more active members, who discuss current European issues and plan public campaigns to promote their ideas. These may range from stimulating political parties and other organisations to focus their attention on European affairs, helping to raise public interest in European elections and organising public demonstrations in favour of European unity. One of the most impressive demonstrations took place during the 1985 Milan Summit meeting when about 100,000 people from all over Europe took part. It has been said that, during the summit meeting, which argued about whether a conference should be convened to negotiate a new treaty for progress to Union, the

Italian Premier turned on the television to show his colleagues the extent of public support for the idea.

Tactics for promoting European unification are various and complementary. Jean Monnet, who set up his Action Committee for the United States of Europe, relied on a small and carefully selected membership of political and trade union leaders to whom he submitted simple and concrete ideas that related to existing circumstances and could be put into effect relatively easily. His method was described as functional, and each step forward flowed from previous advances. Altiero Spinelli, one of the founders of the federalist movement, saw its role as one of persuading the wider public by promoting more populist but also longer-term objectives. But both Monnet and Spinelli saw that the key to their success lay in persuading those with influence and power to support their cause. Indeed, Spinelli's lasting monument to the cause was the blueprint for European Union, in the form of the Draft Treaty which he fathered and shepherded through to its adoption by a massive majority of the first elected European Parliament.

By giving a positive lead at the right time and in the right place, relatively few individuals can achieve major shifts in attitudes and persuade the decision-makers that their efforts will have general support. Time and time again, since the Second World War, committed Europeans have seen their efforts crowned with success. And success brings its own rewards to each active supporter: the feeling that, however humble their role, they will have contributed to shaping history. This is the motive for an ever-swelling number of active protagonists for European unity. It is thanks to their efforts that a United States of Europe will surely come about.

A GLIMPSE AHEAD

But what sort of Europe will it be? If progress towards a European Union by the end of the century is irreversible, then we will soon have an economic and monetary union with a single currency, managed by European institutions. Furthermore, the Union will play a full role in world affairs, with common foreign and defence policies.

The collapse of communism and the dissolution of the Soviet empire have led to most of its former member countries adopting pluralist, democratic market economies. This has laid the foundations for a European Union open to membership of most Central, Eastern and Southern European countries and the development of a growing economic and political interdependence between the Union and Russia as well as other member states of the former Soviet Union.

These dramatic changes have suddenly made the emergence, in the words of Winston Churchill, of 'a kind of United States of Europe' that will include most European countries no longer a dream but a probable development.

What will it be like to live in a United States of Europe? The following imaginary news story in one of Europe's newspapers of the year 2014 will, it is hoped, give an impression of the events and preoccupations likely at the time of a European Presidential Election.

GABRIELLA BY A LANDSLIDE

Brussels, 5 June 2014.

At 11 am the Chief Justice of the European Court formally declared Gabriella Bosconi re-elected President of the United States of Europe. He also confirmed the election of her two team mates, Vice-President Patrick Antrim, who will chair the Council of States, and Vice-President Krystyna Królik, who will preside over the European Parliament's Chamber of the People. The final results gave the three nominees of the Federal People's Party 51 per cent of the votes cast, and their main opponents, the centre-right European Democrat candidates, 37 per cent. The candidates of the Associated National Parties were third with 11 per cent.

The final results were held up by power failures in Romania, which blacked out the transmission of votes to the central polling computer for several hours, and by inevitable delays in getting results transmitted from outlying Anatolian regions of Turkey, where voters had not yet been provided with personal transceivers with which to record their votes directly.

The four-week electoral campaign was dominated by the daily teleconferences, which enabled hundreds of questions to be put to candidates by citizens from all the twenty-eight member states of the Union, as well as by callers from other parts of the world. The issues that dominated the campaign were questions of national identity, conservation of the environment, relations with other parts of the world and the promotion of global security.

Although the re-election of President Bosconi for a second term was never much in doubt, the extent of her victory was surprising. Political commentators attributed it partly to the shrewd choice of her two running mates. Patrick Antrim, the first Protestant Taoiseach of the Irish Federation, brought to the ticket much respect gained from his successful negotiation of the re-unification of Ireland while allowing autonomous Ulster to retain a constitutional link with Britain. Krystyna Królik, who as Polish foreign minister had been the strongest protagonist of the Union's enlargement to the east, carried most of the Eastern European states for her party.

Their principal opponents suffered from having fielded an all-male team. The nationalists, who came a poor third, failed to re-ignite the old campaign for the return of sovereign powers to the states, which were ceded to the Union under the 1998 constitution.

Interviewed by our correspondent after the declaration of the results, President Bosconi gave these answers to the questions put to her.

Q. Much was made during the campaign of the threat to national identity which, it was claimed, could only be safeguarded by the return of sovereign powers to the nation states. Why do you think the nationalists and their cause received such scant support?

Pres. Bosconi: The nationalists confused two distinct issues: the preservation of national cultures and languages and the return of sovereign powers to the states. The Union is committed to protecting and indeed enhancing the identity and integrity of its many nations, which so greatly enrich our common European heritage and culture. During my last administration, over 2 billion Ecu were devoted to programmes protecting ethnic diversity and assisting the development of national cultural activities. We intend to spend even more in the coming years to further these aims. On the other hand, the fully sovereign nation state is surely an anachronism in our interdependent world and most of the electors apparently understood the distinction between pride in one's national identity and state power. Our slogan of 'Unity with Diversity' carried the day.

Q. *Does this mean that you see no future for the continued self-government of our member states?*

Pres. B. On the contrary. After all, our constitution is based on the principle of subsidiarity, which means that the federal government can only exercise those responsibilities which cannot be more effectively dealt with at state, regional or local level. That is why the Union's powers are confined to external and defence affairs, to overall economic and monetary management and to the protection of our common environment. In the social sphere, the bulk of the federal budget is directed towards reducing inequalities in wealth and living standards between the different regions of the Union. While unfettered national sovereignty is now out of date, member states have full autonomy in raising and spending their own taxes. They retain their own legal and educational systems and responsibility for health and social security. Indeed they are responsible for all governmental activities not ceded to the Union or devolved to their regional or local authorities.

Q. *Much concern was voiced during the campaign about the threat to our environment posed by the growing air pollution from the massive increase in road and air transport. What are your plans to deal with these problems?*

Pres. B. As you know we intend to introduce legislation phasing out all internal combustion engines within the next five years and their replacement by the new, extended-range battery-powered electric motors. That will help to deal with air pollution. Easing road and air congestion will be much harder. I hope to form a Commission to examine the problems of traffic congestion and report to us within the next two years.

Q. *To what do you attribute Europe's much improved relations with the countries to the east of our continent and what are your hopes for future global security?*

Pres. B There is little doubt that the establishment twelve years ago of the Eurasian Energy and Environment Agency laid the foundations for the growing economic interdependence between our two continents. War between any of their individual countries is now quite unthinkable in the light of the massive economic benefits we have all reaped from our co-operation and growing interdependence.

On the question of global security, the agreement reached between the USA, Russia, China and ourselves to place all our nuclear weapons under the control of the World Security Authority, so that it can deter any nuclear power from the threat or use of its weapons, has, I believe, removed the spectre of nuclear holocaust from our planet. But now we need to build on that achievement. If war, nuclear or conventional, is to be permanently banished from our planet, then the time has come to plan for a world federation with a common government that would work for the wellbeing and greater prosperity of the whole of mankind. For this grand design the United States of Europe, and the emerging federations in other regions and continents could provide the necessary blueprint.

Appendix

PRINCIPAL FEDERALIST ORGANISATIONS

Federal Union
Federal Trust for Education and Research
(British member of the network of the Trans-European Studies
Association)
Association of World Federalists
The European Movement
all at 158, Buckingham Palace Road, London, SW1W 9TR

Union of European Federalists (UEF)
and
The Young European Federalists (JEF)
(with national, regional and local organisations in some
twenty-two countries)
The European Movement
(international organisation, with National Councils in some
thirty countries)
all at Place du Luxembourg 1, B-1040 Brussels, Belgium)

Association to Unite the Democracies
1506, Pennsylvania Avenue SE, Washington DC 20003, USA

World Federalist Movement
Leliegracht 21, 1016 GR Amsterdam, The Netherlands

Bibliography

Albert, M. and Ball, J. (1983) *Towards European Recovery in the 1980s,* Luxembourg: The European Parliament.

Angell, N. (1908) *The Great Illusion,* London: William Heinemann. (Extracts quoted here are taken from the 1933 edition.)

Boyd Orr, J. (1940) 'Federalism and science', in Channing-Pearce, M. (ed.) *Federal Union,* London: Jonathan Cape.

Brett, R. (1992) *Papers in the Theory and Practice of Human Rights* Nos 1 and 2, Colchester: University of Essex.

Budd, A. (1987) *The EEC – A Guide to the Maze,* 2nd edn, London: Kogan Page.

Burgess, M. (1989) *Federalism and European Union,* London: Routledge.

Burrows, B., Denton, G. and Edwards, G. (eds) (1978) *Federal Solutions to European Issues,* London: Macmillan.

Butler, M. (1986) *Europe : More than a Continent,* London: Heinemann.

Cecchini, P. (1988) *The European Challenge 1992,* Aldershot: Wildwood House.

Centre for Economic Policy Research (1992) *Is Bigger Better? The Economics of EC Enlargement,* London: CEPR.

—— (1922) *The Association Process: Making it Work,* London: CEPR.

Coudenhove-Kalergi, R. (1966) *Pan-Europa,* 3rd edn, Vienna: Pan-Europa Verlag. (Originally published in 1923.)

Curry, W. B. (1939) *The case for Federal Union,* London, Harmondsworth: Penguin.

EC Commission (1970a) *Economic and Monetary Union* (Werner Report), Luxembourg: EC Bulletin.

—— (1970b) *Problems of Political Unification* (Davignon Report), Luxembourg: EC Bulletin.

—— (1976) *European Union* (Tindemans Report), Luxembourg: EC Bulletin.

—— (1977a) *Role of Public Finance on European Integration* (MacDougall Report), Brussels: European Communities.

—— (1977b) *Treaties establishing the European Communities,* abridged version, Luxembourg: European Communities.

—— (1981) *Draft European Act* (Genscher–Colombo Report), Luxembourg: EC Bulletin.

—— (1985a) *A People's Europe* (Addonino Report), Luxembourg: European Communities

—— (1985b) *Completing the Internal Market* (Cockfield White Paper), Luxembourg: European Communities.

—— (1986) *Single European Act,* Luxembourg: EC Bulletin.

—— (1987) *A Strategy for the Evolution of the Economic System of the EC* (Padoa-Schoppia Report), Brussels: European Communities

—— (1990) *The Community Charter of Fundamental Social Rights for Workers,* Luxembourg: European Communities

European Communities (1992) *Treaty on European Union,* London: HMSO.

European Parliament (1984) *Draft Treaty establishing the European Union,* Luxembourg: European Parliament

Federal Trust for Education and Research (1991) *Europe's Future: Four Scenarios,* London: FTER.

Heath, E. (1988) *European Unity over the Next Ten Years: from Community to Union* (Lothian Memorial Lecture), London: Royal Institute of International Affairs.

Hoggart, R. and Johnson, D. (1987) *An Idea of Europe,* London: Chatto & Windus.

Laffan, B. (1992) *Integration and Cooperation in Europe,* London: Routledge.

Layton, C. (1986) *One Europe: One World,* London: Journal of World Trade Law.

—— (1989) *A Step Beyond Fear,* London: Federal Trust for Education and Research.

Leonard, D. (1988) *Pocket Guide to the European Community,* Oxford: Blackwell.

Lipgens, W. (1986) *Documents on the History of European Integration,* New York: Walter de Gruyter.

Mayne R. and Pinder, J. with Roberts, J. (1990) *Federal Union: The Pioneers,* London: Macmillan.

McInnes, C. (ed.) (1992) *Security and Strategy in the New Europe,* London: Routledge.

Michalski, A. and Wallace, H. (1992) *The European Community: The Challenge of Enlargement,* London: Royal Institute of International Affairs.

Monnet, J. (1976) *Memoirs,* trans. R. Mayne (1978), London: William Collins.

Pelkmans, J. and Winters, A. (1988) *Europe's Domestic Market,* London: Routledge.

Pinder, J. (1991) *The European Community and Eastern Europe,* London: Royal Institute of International Affairs and Pinter.

—— (1992) *European Community,* Oxford: Oxford University Press.

Pryce, R. (ed.) (1987) *The Dynamics of European Union,* London: Croom Helm.

Robbins, L. (1939) *The Economic Causes of War,* London: Jonathan Cape.

Royal Institute of International Affairs (1988) *Europe's Future in Space,* London: Routledge & Kegan Paul.

Sharp, M. and Shearman, C. (1987) *European Technological Cooperation*, London: Routledge & Kegan Paul.

Sidjanski, D. (1992) *L'Avenir Fédéraliste de L'Europe*, Geneva: Presses Universitaires de France.

Streit, C. (1939) *Union Now: A Proposal for a Federal Union of the Democracies of the North Atlantic*, London and New York: Jonathan Cape and Harper.

Vandame, J. (ed.) (1985) *New Dimensions in European Social Policy*, London: Croom Helm.

Vile, M.J.C. (1973) *Federalism in the United States, Canada and Australia*, Research Papers 2, Commission on the Constitution, London: HMSO.

Wistrich, E. (1989) *After 1992*, London: Routledge.

Index